Can I Keep Drinking?

The dominant US perspective about drinking problems—that abstinence is the only genuine solution—gets a thorough re-examination in *Can I Keep Drinking?* If you're looking for a fresh and evidence-based perspective on drinking problems and ways to change them, everything you need to know is here.

—**Tom Horvath, Ph.D., ABPP**, President, Practical Recovery
Author: *Sex, Drugs, Gambling & Chocolate:*
A Workbook for Overcoming Addictions

Can I Keep Drinking? is a fresh voice in the emerging field of moderation treatment programs, which claim that abstinence-only approaches to problem drinking represent a "one size fits all" that clearly do not fit all drinkers. This book comes alongside the reader who is brave enough to ask the honest question *Can I keep drinking?* and offers practical, real-world answers that will guide them into having a healthier relationship with alcohol, regardless of where they fall on the spectrum.

—**Gabrielle Glaser**, Author: *Her Best-Kept Secret:*
Why Women Drink—And How They Can Regain Control

When someone faces the notion that they may have an alcohol problem for the first time, it is almost impossible to know where to begin. *Can I Keep Drinking?* offers a practical, thorough, easy-to-read roadmap for addressing this issue.

—**Kevin P. Hill, MD, MHS**,
Addiction Psychiatrist, Clinical Researcher
Author: *Marijuana: The Unbiased Truth*
about the World's Most Popular Weed

Cyndi Turner explains the foundations of moderate drinking empathetically and intelligently. This book is an excellent addition to the harm reduction canon, one that will certainly help readers navigate a healthier relationship with alcohol.

—**Kelsey Osgood**, Moderation Management facilitator
Author: *How to Disappear Completely: On Modern Anorexia*

Thorough, well-organized, and compassionate…Reveals Ms. Turner's deep experience and understanding of the processes one goes through in struggling with a relationship with alcohol. She illuminates the spectrum of alcohol use and provides concrete, specific criteria to help you determine for yourself exactly where you may fall along that spectrum. More importantly, she also provides the resources and behavioral changes to help you regain control of your relationship with alcohol without necessarily eliminating it from your life.

—**Jim**, client

Cyndi Turner's methods, analysis, and perspective have changed my life physically and emotionally. Thinking outside of traditional therapies she has helped me be "present" and embrace every minute and moment of my life.

—**Alberto**, client

Can I Keep Drinking?

HOW YOU CAN DECIDE
WHEN ENOUGH IS ENOUGH

Cyndi Turner, LCSW, LSATP

NEW YORK

NASHVILLE   MELBOURNE

Can I Keep Drinking?

HOW YOU CAN DECIDE WHEN ENOUGH IS ENOUGH

Published in New York, New York, by Morgan James Publishing. Morgan James and The Entrepreneurial Publisher are trademarks of Morgan James, LLC. www.MorganJamesPublishing.com

The Morgan James Speakers Group can bring authors to your live event. For more information or to book an event visit The Morgan James Speakers Group at www.TheMorganJamesSpeakersGroup.com.

Shelfie

A **free** eBook edition is available with the purchase of this print book.

CLEARLY PRINT YOUR NAME ABOVE IN UPPER CASE

Instructions to claim your free eBook edition:
1. Download the Shelfie app for Android or iOS
2. Write your name in **UPPER CASE** above
3. Use the Shelfie app to submit a photo
4. Download your eBook to any device

ISBN 978-1-63047-989-3 paperback
ISBN 978-1-63047-991-6 eBook
ISBN 978-1-63047-990-9 hardcover
Library of Congress Control Number:
2016903704

Cover Design by:
Chris Treccani
www.3dogdesign.net

Interior Design by:
Bonnie Bushman
The Whole Caboodle Graphic Design

In an effort to support local communities, raise awareness and funds, Morgan James Publishing donates a percentage of all book sales for the life of each book to

Habitat for Humanity Peninsula and Greater Williamsburg.
Get involved today! Visit
www.MorganJamesBuilds.com

Thank you to my girls, Kaitlyn and Jacklyn, for being patient with "Book Mommy," who was not much fun.

And to my husband—without you none of this would have been possible.

This is for all of the clients who have shared their stories, struggles, and successes with me over the last twenty years. I admire your courageousness to admit to a problem, your willingness to evaluate yourself, and your commitment to try new ways of approaching life. A little part of you is written on these pages. You inspire me.

Contents

Foreword

Jason R. Kilmer, PhD,
University of Washington
Assistant Director of Health & Wellness for Alcohol and Other Drug Education
Division of Student Life
Associate Professor
Psychiatry & Behavioral Sciences

Diane E. Logan, PhD
Clinical Psychologist
West Hawaii Mental Health Center

"How do I know if I drink too much?" As individuals with expertise in addictive behaviors research, consultation, and clinical work, we hear this question quite frequently. You may have asked it about yourself or someone you know. The challenge is that knowing someone drinks alcohol, or even knowing how much alcohol they drink, tells us very little.

Context matters so much.

Imagine we know someone drinks three cans of beer while watching a late football game on TV. Is that a concern? It depends on context. Is that person taking sleeping medication prior to going to bed? If so, that opens up big concerns related to drug interactions.

Imagine we know someone drinks two cocktails with dinner, and imagine we even control for what counts as "one drink" (something you'll learn about in this book). Is that a concern? It depends on context. Is that person home for the day after work, or is that person about to go out and start a shift driving a vehicle?

Imagine we know someone drinks one small glass of wine with their partner before bed each night. Is that a concern? It depends on context. Is that person struggling to control their blood sugar levels in the morning? If so, that medical condition may be made worse by what appears to be a minimal amount of alcohol.

Alcohol is a substance associated with everything from cultural ceremonies to celebrations to complementing meals—ranging from a bratwurst/beer combination to a top-shelf cocktail in a fine restaurant. We see it at sporting events, restaurants, bars, and, increasingly, theaters, concerts, and other settings. But, just like the variety of people in these settings, each individual brings a different life story, situation, and history to the table. Each individual can be in the same place, and even drinking the same drink, but they could all be drinking in a different context based on where they are in their lives.

From a legal standpoint, keep in mind that if you're under twenty-one, it's illegal to drink. If the main alcohol-related harm you're trying to avoid has to do with legal issues, choosing to abstain makes the most sense. From a medical standpoint, many conditions are worsened by any alcohol consumption, and again choosing to abstain may be the safest route.

That said, you are the expert on your present context and how alcohol fits into your life. But sometimes those around us see patterns that are more difficult for us to see ourselves. Think of a hiker in a forest—she is the expert on her immediate surroundings (context), but it's more difficult for her to see the entire path of where she started and where she is going (pattern). By picking up *Can I Keep Drinking?*, you are likely considering a change or working with someone who is considering a change. That contemplation of change, something you'll also learn about in this book, is an important step in deciding what works best for you. If someone recommended this book to you, maybe a friend or therapist, that person may have a bird's-eye view of a pattern they hope you'll explore.

Can I Keep Drinking? is thoughtfully written to highlight the choices you have, and to allow you to assess what might be best for you given your unique context and pattern. This book might be enough for you to make some pretty big changes, or you might need some additional consultation and help as a complement to the efforts you are making. Regardless, you know yourself best.

We write this foreword as a team who has collaborated on a number of research studies about alcohol, and science can be applied to whatever direction you are considering. Approach any change you are making like an experiment. When we conduct experiments, we have a prediction, or hypothesis, and conduct our experiment to see if that hypothesis is supported or not. No matter the outcome, we still learn something. You can approach behavior change around alcohol use the same way.

If you set a goal of three drinks on a given night, and meet that goal, congratulations! Step back, pat yourself on the back, and consider how you were able to approach that situation so you can replicate that success on subsequent days.

If you set a goal of three drinks and wind up drinking more than that, there's a chance to consider what you can learn from that situation. What worked? What didn't work so well? What happened that you didn't see coming? What could you do differently next time to meet your goal?

We both trained with Dr. Alan Marlatt, who made huge contributions to the addictive behaviors field with his work around harm reduction and relapse prevention. Alan passed away in 2011, representing a significant personal loss to us and a major professional loss to the field. Alan used to talk about "Apparently Irrelevant Decisions." What are these? They are the little things a person does that, on their own, seem pretty innocent, but actually set a person up for a slip or a lapse when they have a particular goal. What is an example? A person who is trying to avoid drinking knows that a trigger for drinking heavily is being angry, and decides to call an ex-partner to see how things are going. Probably not surprisingly, they get in an argument, the person gets angry, and the person winds up drinking. Calling an ex is an apparently irrelevant decision. On its own, it seems fairly innocent: "Hey, I was just checking in to say hi!" Instead, it likely set the person up for a lapse.

This phenomenon is not unique to alcohol. If you're trying to watch what you eat, think about the food purchases you make when you go to the grocery store hungry as opposed to after a filling meal. When are you more likely to stick to the grocery list you brought? How does a person overcome these? Well, there's no magic wand, but decisions like these are sometimes easier to see as a pattern first, and then the context can be examined for clues.

Can I Keep Drinking? provides a chance to walk through a range of options so that you can decide what works best for you given the context and the pattern in which your drinking occurs. And just like a science experiment, it gives you a chance to change (or choose not to), learn from the outcome, and reset your compass as needed. Your direction might be the same as the next person who reads this book, or it might be completely different.

Regardless of what you decide, remember you are not alone in your choice. Many people choose every day to not drink at all. Many people choose every day to continue to drink the same amount. Many people choose every day to drink less. If you're unsure, you may already have people in your life who can help you decide, such as relatives, friends, and professionals including medical and behavioral health providers. If you don't, consider that many people find it helpful to get an outside opinion, and consultations with a professional can help you make those decisions. But in the end, the choice is yours. We hope *Can I Keep Drinking?* is a helpful resource in deciding what to do next.

Preface

This book is written as if you were sitting in a nonjudgmental therapy session with a twenty-year expert in the field (me!) who realizes that one size of treatment does not fit all. While all people share certain universal experiences, there are many ways to look at and solve the problems that arise in the human experience. I believe, in one sense, that you are the expert because it is your life, but in another sense, I am the expert because it is *not* my life. My emotions are not involved, so I am able to have a better perspective. I have no agenda other than helping you be the best version of yourself that you can be—healthy, happy, and balanced.

"Can I keep drinking?" you may ask. This is a very complicated question to answer. My goal is to share with you the steps that I take my clients through in order to figure this out. You may be wondering if your drinking is out of control, or you may have a family member who is unhappy with your current drinking patterns or behavior. Basically, in these following pages, you are getting a lot of the information that I would share with someone during six to nine months of group and individual therapy.

I have developed the "How Do I Know If I Can Keep Drinking? Quiz" to help you answer this very question. It is personalized to your specific experiences and goals. Based upon your answers, you can determine whether or not you can safely keep drinking. I will also help you understand the various predicators for success or failure. You may be tempted to skip ahead and take the quiz, but I recommend that you get some information first. I believe that my job as a therapist is not to make the decision for you, but to give you information so that you can make the best decision for yourself.

What you will get from me is all the book knowledge I have learned over my twenty-year career (yawn), but more importantly, the examples, trials, and successes of many people who have tried to moderate their drinking. You are not alone in this struggle. Once you have completed this book, you will have a better sense of whether you have a drinking problem and whether you are able to safely drink again. Most of the data provided in this book concerns adults over the age of twenty-one in the United States, but I have also provided information about the impact of drinking in adolescence as well as in other countries around the world.

When a client or family member calls and asks me if their spouse, child, family member, or friend can keep drinking, I tell them honestly that I don't know. It would be wrong for me to make the assumption that just because someone is having a current issue with drinking, they are therefore an alcoholic and can never drink again. Anyone can keep drinking—it's a matter of whether they *should* keep drinking.

I want you to have pertinent information so you can decide if it is time to make a change in your life regarding alcohol. I am giving you tools to find solutions that work for you. Your goal will be to turn your insights into action. Read ahead to find out how to have a better relationship with alcohol.

Acknowledgments

I want to acknowledge everyone who reviewed the many early versions of my manuscript: Daddy, who took the time to read it while recovering from oral surgery; Mike, who ran the household while I was writing; Kaitlyn, who is the smartest fourteen- year-old I know; Craig, who gave me unwavering support in every step of this process; and Kelsey Osgood, who gave me the Moderation Management perspective . . . and noticed just how many incorrect hyphens I was using. Jacklyn, your witty humor kept me laughing throughout this process.

Thank you to the following literary agents: Rita Rosenkranz, for polishing my query; Jill Marsal, for reworking my proposal; Michael Ebling, for opening some doors; and Michaela Hamilton, for initiating the next steps.

Thank you to my team at Morgan James Publishing: David Hancock, Jim Howard, Dave Sauer, Angie Kiesling, Nickcole Watkins, and Tiffany Gibson.

Special thanks to my business partner, Craig James, who handled all the graphics and computer issues, for which I just do not have the patience.

Introduction

Get Ready for Change

Approximately 80 percent of treatment programs offer abstinence-only approaches, but mine is not one of them. Substance abuse, including alcohol abuse, is the only disease that some professionals believe must be treated only when the person is without symptoms. There are multiple paths to abusing substances; therefore, there should be multiple paths to recovery. One size does not fit all. Treatment providers should strive to create a therapeutic alliance with their clients, agree on goals, establish each other's roles, and create a bond. In this book, we will work together to answer the question *Can I keep drinking?*

What other disease requires a person to be totally free of the problem to receive help? I don't think this requirement is fair. I do not turn away people from receiving treatment if they are still drinking. I know that when they finally make that first call to me, they have probably just experienced a crisis and are at one of the lowest points in their struggle with alcohol. It would be insane to deny them help because they are in the midst of their problem and experiencing symptoms. For drinkers, the most recognizable symptom is drinking. How crazy is it, then, to turn people away because they are exhibiting the symptoms of heavy drinking?

I start therapy wherever people are and develop a personalized treatment plan for them. This is what this book is designed to do: help you figure out the impact that drinking has had on your life and determine what a healthier relationship with alcohol might be for you.

The first chapter supports the reality that not everybody who drinks has a problem with alcohol. In fact, only a very small percentage of the population should actually be classified as alcoholics. I review who is drinking in the world, focusing mainly on data compiled in the United States. There are many types of drinkers. The *spectrum of alcohol use* explores the different types of drinkers and helps you figure out where you fit.

Chapter 2 challenges current treatment models and perceptions about drinkers. Many treatment facilities, therapists, self-help groups, courts, and legal systems believe that all problem drinkers are alcoholics and therefore can never safely drink again. This is inaccurate and is often one of the main reasons why nine out of ten problem drinkers do not receive the help necessary to improve the quality of their lives. This chapter also begins to explore the concept of moderate drinking. Moderate drinking is considered no more than two drinks a day for men and one drink a day for women, where the goal is not to change mood, and where there are no consequences to the drinker or their loved ones.

The third chapter provides an opportunity to self-assess. The new diagnostic criteria in the *Diagnostic and Statistical Manual 5* are included. Based upon your reported symptoms, you can determine if you meet the criteria for a mild, moderate, or severe alcohol use disorder, using the same tool that clinicians and medical professionals use. By admitting and understanding the impact that alcohol has had on your life, you can then determine if you should make some changes to your current drinking patterns.

Chapter 4 provides practical information about the impact of alcohol on your body. You will learn that drinking impacts every organ in the body, including the brain. Special attention is given to the heart, liver, pancreas, immune system, brain, and pregnancy. We also look at the relationship between alcohol and driving accidents. Alcohol use is often chronic, progressive, and, in extreme cases, fatal. Withdrawal from alcohol can be fatal and should be medically supervised.

In chapter 5, you will read about Prochaska and DiClemente's *Stages of Change model*. This model explores whether you are ready to make changes to your alcohol use. However, you first need to figure out where you are before you can move forward. Many client examples will demonstrate how others have moved forward in the process and will help you figure out how to help yourself or a loved one. The *cost/benefit paradigm of drinking* is then introduced and challenges treatment to focus on the benefits of drinking and the costs to not drinking rather than the traditional emphasis on why people should stop drinking.

Chapter 6 is the chapter that most people dread. In this chapter, I encourage you to remain alcohol free for a set period of time. Being alcohol free for a period of time will afford you better clarity to identify the pros and cons of your drinking. I review the reasons why I actually want you to feel some emotional discomfort so that you can come up with solutions to deal with it. I never ask people to make a change without giving them the tools to make the change, and I will do that here in this chapter. I will show you how to manage cravings, thoughts, emotions, and situations without turning to alcohol. I will help you discover healthier ways to deal with life and develop alternative ways to have fun and deal with boredom.

In chapter 7, you will take the "How Do I Know if I Can Keep Drinking? Quiz." Interpretations are given for a range of responses. Based on your answers, I will give you predictions on whether you should develop a *moderate drinking plan*.

In chapter 8, you will develop a moderate drinking plan based on your specific goals. Tools such as positive and negative tangible reminders, what to say when asked if you want a drink, and ways to monitor the plan are reviewed. A gut check regarding intent, impact, amount, and frequency is explained.

Chapter 9 includes the booklet "Relapse Reality: Understanding Myths in Dual Diagnosis Treatment." This chapter clarifies mistaken beliefs associated with recovery. It also features practical tools to maintain your recovery, whether your goal is to keep drinking as you always have, to drink moderately, or to maintain abstinence.

The final chapter explores the many paths to recovery. I have included resources for the different types of treatment available. Most people are familiar with Alcoholics Anonymous and the concept of rehab but know nothing of anything in between. I have thus included treatment options including inpatient and outpatient programs, types of professionals, medications, as well as no-cost self-help groups and online recovery resources.

Throughout this book I have included "Interesting Info." These are little-known factoids regarding alcohol and drinking. Have fun sounding smart with this alcohol trivia!

So here are my thoughts on whether you can keep drinking...

Chapter 1

Not Everybody Who Drinks Has A Problem

*T*he next time you are in a group, look around. Of the twelve ladies in your book club, one of them may drink too much and has family members who are worried about her.

Two of the forty people in the train on the way to work are likely alcoholics.

One of the parents on your son's soccer team may have had a blackout last night.

Three of the roommates living on your floor in the college dorm may already have or are developing a serious drinking problem.

Six of the people in your neighborhood of one hundred houses may be considering leaving their spouses because of their spouses' drinking.

Two of your friends in your small country club may still have an adult child living at home because they can't hold down a job as a result of their alcohol use.

While sitting in Sunday services, eight of the three hundred parishioners present may be praying for a resolution to their alcohol problems.

Meanwhile, over a third of the people in the aforementioned scenarios never drink alcohol at all. Around half of the others occasionally open a bottle of red wine, but it goes bad because they forget all about it. When they go to a restaurant, sometimes they order a cocktail, while other times they order a soda.

Which one are you? What are you willing to do about it?

This first chapter will review who is drinking. While much of the data is focused on the population of the United States, it can theoretically apply to any developed country where alcohol is part of the social norm. In fact, the United States is only thirty-second on the list of the world's top alcohol-consuming countries.

The World Health Organization (WHO) has found that nine of the top ten alcohol-consuming countries are located in Eastern Europe. These nations include Russia, Hungary, and Belarus, among others. They also found that five of these countries had the highest prevalence of alcohol-use disorders, supporting the fact that the more people drink, the more problems they have.

The WHO suspects that one reason for the excessive drinking and its ensuing problems in these countries is that their citizens lack sufficient public health awareness to make informed decisions about their alcohol use. The WHO also notes that many of these countries do not have public policy initiatives to address the effects of alcohol use on the general public. Nonetheless, regardless of any one nation's drinking age, income level, or years of education, alcohol problems are found all over the world, not just in America.

Let's take a look and define the different types of alcohol users.

Who Is Drinking in the United States?

The 2015 United States Census Bureau recorded approximately 323 million people living in the United States. The National Institutes of Health report that approximately 1 in 12 people has a substance use disorder, and around 6 percent of people have a serious problem with alcohol. That's 19 million people—enough people to fill the entire state of Florida!

Here's an even more overwhelming number. It is estimated that about 30 percent of people have some degree of a problem with alcohol. These people are not necessarily alcoholics and may not meet diagnostic criteria, but drinking has caused some problem in their lives. This is an astounding number—over 90 million people. That's the same number of people who live in the Central Time Zone!

Spectrum of Alcohol Use

Whenever I begin a substance-use-disorders evaluation, I let my clients and their family members know that I believe in a spectrum of alcohol use. Not everyone who drinks alcohol is an alcoholic, and certainly not everyone who drinks has a drinking problem. Most people fall on a continuum of alcohol use throughout their lifespans. An increase in alcohol use is typically gradual. No one becomes an alcoholic on his or her first sip. Alcohol abuse is often chronic, progressive, and, in some cases, fatal.

Experimental Use: This first stage is often driven by curiosity of what alcohol does and what it tastes like. This often occurs during the teenage years. First-time alcohol users often want to see what all the fuss is about. After trying alcohol, some people decide they can take it or leave it. Others will have too much, pray to the "porcelain god," and not drink again for a long period of time, having gained a better understanding of their limits.

A very small percentage of first-time drinkers will describe their first intoxication as "meeting my best friend," "finding the answer to my problems," or "something I couldn't wait to do again." This population has experienced not only the chemical change associated with alcohol, but also a physiological rush. Dr. Nora Volkow, head of the National Institute on Drug Abuse since 2003, describes this as a hijacking of the brain. It is like flipping a switch in the brain, and it affords no retreat for the addict. This group of drinkers will often go on to experience addiction if their alcohol use continues. The experimental use of alcohol becomes dangerous when curiosity is quenched, yet the person returns for more.

Occasional Use: Occasional users are not preoccupied with drinking, but they will often drink in social situations. Adults may consume alcohol when they go out to eat, attend a party, celebrate an important event, or want to relax on some weekends. Teenagers may consume alcohol as part of an event like homecoming, prom, or a concert. This type of drinking is often not a problem; however, younger drinkers tend to drink more for effect and to binge drink to become intoxicated. This increases the odds for poor decision making and cell adaptation. We will address this concern more in chapter 7.

Situational Use: Situational use is also not usually a problem. However, the amount and frequency of alcohol use begins to increase. What was once special-occasion drinking now becomes more consistent and associated with specific events such as every weekend, parties, birthdays, sporting events, clubs, and other such things.

Binge Use: A binge drinker is someone who consumes a large quantity of alcohol, usually five or more drinks in two hours for men and four or more drinks for women, with the intent of becoming intoxicated. Bingeing can be a part of normal experimentation. The person who experiences the consequences of drinking too much and refrains from use for a period of time will most likely not develop a problem, but the problem drinker will experience the consequence yet do the same thing the very next night, weekend, or party. Note the difference between sipping from a red cup at a party or social event versus drinking to get drunk. Binge use is often the start of problem use. While the binge drinker's frequency tends to be somewhat sporadic, the amount consumed is usually large.

Alcohol Abuse: This consumption pattern tends not to occur every day and is not a problem every time a person drinks; however, it is beginning to cause problems. Normal drinkers will slow down or stop drinking when they have had a fight, developed a health problem, or received a legal charge. People who abuse alcohol tend to continue their drinking patterns despite having recurrent problems. A good way to define alcohol abuse is this:

If it causes a problem, it is a problem.

The person who abuses alcohol tends to drink in a larger amount than others and does so more frequently. However, at this stage, many people either minimize the existence of a problem or deny alcohol's impact. They may say such things as "I can stop anytime I want," "It's not like I drink every day," or "I'm not as bad as _____."

Alcohol Dependence: At this stage, alcohol use has become a serious problem, and we describe the person as an alcoholic. This person tends to drink on a very regular basis and in large quantities. The alcohol has changed body chemistry, and the person has developed a tolerance to it, meaning increasing amounts are necessary to achieve the same effect. This person may also experience withdrawal symptoms if denied alcohol, physiological responses such as delirium tremens (the shakes), seizures, hallucinations, delusions, heart attack, and stroke. These are dangerous, can be life threatening, and require medical attention.

INTERESTING INFO: Did you know that withdrawal from alcohol could kill you? Many people mistakenly believe that coming off painkillers, stimulants, or heroin can be fatal. It generally is not. These withdrawals are extremely painful, with the acute symptoms lasting for several days, possibly up to a week. One client coming off painkillers said, "I did not know I could feel that bad and not be dead."

Alcohol is a central nervous system depressant. CNS depressants, often referred to as sedatives or tranquilizers, slow brain activity. This is why when people drink, they feel more relaxed and do not filter their thoughts, actions, or words as well. When a person no longer has alcohol in the body, the CNS begins to experience a rebound effect that can result in potentially life-threatening complications.

On one end of the spectrum of use are people who do not drink at all. In fact, more than 35 percent of people do not drink any alcohol at all. Does that surprise you? Some people just don't like the effect, feel out of control when drinking, have had a family member with a drinking problem, don't want the calories, or feel it is against their religious beliefs or negatively affects their health.

Moving from left to right on the spectrum, we next come to the 20 percent who engage in normal experimentation with alcohol. Some teenagers and early twenty-year-olds try alcohol and decide drinking is not for them. Others like the effect and continue their consumption.

Drinking at this stage often occurs as part of a social experience, such as attending a party or commemorating an event like a birthday, fraternity rush, graduation, or other such events.

In the middle part of the spectrum are the individuals who drink too much or drink on a regular basis. They may drink in college, in early adulthood, after a breakup, in a crisis period, or because of grief. Most people in this part of the spectrum recognize that their drinking, either the amount or the frequency, is getting out of control and can make some behavioral and lifestyle changes to bring it back to a non-detrimental level. But the National Institute on Alcohol Abuse and Alcoholism (NIAAA) estimates that about 28 percent of adults drink at levels that put them at risk for alcohol dependence and alcohol-related problems.

Moving into the third quarter of the spectrum, we see what used to be called "alcohol abusers." In chapter 3, we will review the changes to how we now diagnose substance-use disorders. These are the people whose drinking may be causing problems in their lives. They may not drink every day, and they may not have a problem every time they drink, but their drinking is problematic. This middle-to-end area of the spectrum includes about 22 percent of the population.

Only a very small percentage of the population, about 6 percent, is physically dependent on alcohol. These people are what most nondrinkers, drinkers, and treatment providers picture when they think of someone with a drinking problem. This 6 percent may be the ones you compare yourself to in order to validate that you do not have a drinking problem. This small percentage includes people who drink every day, need alcohol to function, have suffered severe consequences like DUIs (driving under the influence), and have lost something of importance or value to them—spouse, child, job, house, or health. My frustration on behalf of problem drinkers who are not chemically dependent on alcohol is that they are compared to and receive treatment more appropriate for this relatively small percentage. I will address this more in chapter 2.

We may vacillate on the spectrum of alcohol use over our lifetimes. What causes a problem at one time of our lives may not be an issue in another. For example, many twentysomethings drink more than people in their forties. Does this mean they are all alcoholics? No. A twenty-five-year-old typically does not have as many responsibilities as a forty-year-old. A twenty-five-year-old can stay out late on the weekend as long as he doesn't make unhealthy decisions when out and gets a ride home if necessary. However, if a forty-year-old stays out until three in the morning, he may neglect his spouse, kids, lawn, or household chores.

The period from the late teens and into the twenties is usually a developmental stage where individuals are typically experiencing life, dating to find a mate, and figuring out their life goals and pleasures. This age group will naturally socialize and come in contact with more people than do other age groups. Alcohol may often be a part of this socialization. Individuals in their early- to mid-twenties should also be learning more about their strengths and weaknesses, solidifying their identities, and developing appropriate coping skills. If they accomplish these tasks, they will be less likely to develop an alcohol problem even though their consumption rates may be higher than older individuals'.

The Substance Abuse and Mental Health Services Administration (SAMHSA) discovered the following:

- 46 percent of those 18 to 20 years old have consumed alcohol at least once.
- 69 percent of those 21 to 25 years old drink at least several times a year.
- Almost 75 percent of those 12 to 20 years old have not used alcohol in the last month.

Though it is true that a large proportion of young adults are drinking, it does not mean they all have a drinking problem. Nonetheless, some of the young adults I work with justify their alcohol use by saying, "Everyone drinks." These statistics, however, show that in fact not everyone is drinking.

It is important to note that the above numbers include drinkers across the entire spectrum of alcohol use. Some might have had just 1 drink in the last month, while others may have had multiple drinks a day. In fact, only 12 percent of people ages 18 to 25 reported heavy drinking (having 5 or more drinks for 5 of the last 30 days).

SAMHSA puts out a National Survey on Drug Use and Health (NSDUH). The information below comes from their report that was published in 2015.

- There are approximately 323 million people in the United States. Of that population, 139.7 million are current alcohol users ages 12 or older.

- Of these drinkers, 22 percent are *binge drinkers*. A binge drinker is someone who consumes a large quantity of alcohol, usually 5 or more drinks within 2 hours for men and 4 or more drinks for women, with the intent of becoming intoxicated.

- Another 6.2 percent are defined as *heavy drinkers*. Heavy drinkers are men who drink more than 15 drinks per week and women who have more than 8 per week. *Heavy drinking* is also considered binge drinking if engaged in for 5 or more of the last 30 days. More men (9.5 percent) than women (3.3 percent) are defined as heavy drinkers. This is the group of people we usually call alcoholics.

- Approximately 37 percent of people drink within normal limits. They have 1 or 2 drinks on an occasional basis and experience no negative consequences.

- Another 19 percent of the population consumes more drinks each episode or on more days of the week. Only 9 percent drink both more each day and a larger amount.
- *Social drinker* is the commonly accepted term for the person who drinks on occasion. There are no negative consequences to their use. No one complains about how much they drink or when they drink. Alcohol is rarely on their mind, they do not lose control when they drink, and they don't set a limit on how much they drink because they have not needed to do so.

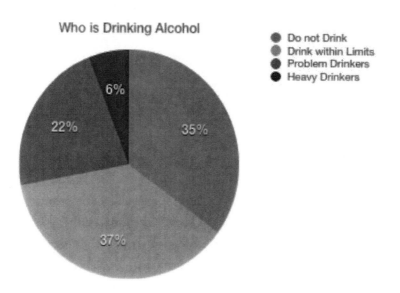

Who is Drinking Alcohol

- Do not Drink
- Drink within Limits
- Problem Drinkers
- Heavy Drinkers

6%
22%
35%
37%

Do these numbers surprise you? Keep in mind that who we spend our time with reflects what we believe is normal. If you are spending a lot of time in happy hours at bars, you will think that most people drink. If you hang out with people who party a lot, you will think drinking is normal. If your parents ended their day with a cocktail, you will think this is how it's done. If every holiday, celebration, or get-together involves drinking, this becomes normal for you. If your answer to the question *Can I get you a drink?* usually involves alcohol, you may have a problem. What about water, tea, soda, coffee, or juice?

Which type of drinker are you? Why?

_____

_____

_____

Has there been a period in your life when you drank more? What was going on at that time?

_____

_____

_____

There are many points along the spectrum of alcohol use where you may develop a problem. And sometimes, as the environment changes, your drinking pattern changes. This can be for either good or bad. With conscious effort, you may be able to alter your drinking pattern, amount, and frequency to move to a safer end of the spectrum. That is what this book is about: figuring out the answer to the question *Can I keep drinking?*

INTERESTING INFO: Did you know that saliva regenerates every ten to fifteen minutes? Why is this important? Police and treatment providers know this. The excuses of "I just used mouthwash" or "I took some cough syrup" are not accurate explanations for testing positive for alcohol on a breath test. A person would have to actually drink the mouthwash or consume a large quantity of cold medicine to register positive. Initially, a Breathalyzer would read very high if a person had just used mouthwash or taken cough syrup, but then fifteen minutes later, nothing readable would remain—unless the person had drunk it. Just don't drive after you drink. Then you won't have to worry about making up excuses.

ANOTHER ROUND OF CHAPTER 1
Not Everybody Who Drinks Has a Problem

- Over a lifetime, individuals may vacillate on the spectrum of alcohol use.
- The stages on the spectrum include the following:
  - ° Experimental use
  - ° Occasional use
  - ° Situational use
  - ° Binge use
  - ° Alcohol abuse
  - ° Alcohol dependence
- Not all drinkers are alcoholics, but if drinking causes a problem, it is a problem.
- Nearly 35 percent of the population above the age of 12 does not drink at all.
- Around 28 percent of American adults drink at levels that put them at risk for alcohol-related problems.
- About 37 percent of the population are social drinkers who do not experience problems from their use.
- 22 percent of the population are binge drinkers who consume a large quantity of alcohol (5 or more drinks within 2 hours for men and 4 or more drinks for women) with the intent of becoming intoxicated.
- 6 percent of the population are heavy drinkers, consuming more than 15 drinks per week for men and more than 8 drinks for women.
- Heavy drinkers are typically those we refer to as alcoholics.

Chapter 2

Why Are All Alcohol Users Treated The Same?

I   *f there are so few alcoholics, why are all drinkers treated the same?*
This is a great question. According to the National Institute
on Alcohol Abuse and Alcoholism (NIAAA) and other
public health agencies, there are at least four times as many drinkers
experiencing problems as alcoholics in this country. However, most
alcohol-treatment programs are designed for the most severe drinkers,
the ones typically called alcoholics. Many people avoid seeking help
because they do not want to be labeled as an alcoholic, attend Alcoholics
Anonymous (AA) meetings, or accept abstinence as the sole goal of
treatment. Giving up drinking is not the only answer for dealing with
alcohol-related problems.

A 2014 collaborative study between the Centers for Disease
Control and Prevention and the Substance Abuse Mental Health
Services Administration (SAMHSA) explored the prevalence of alcohol

dependence among drinkers in the United States. The study found that binge drinking and alcohol dependence were most common among men aged 18 to 24. Binge drinking was most prevalent in families with incomes of $75,000 or more. Interestingly, alcohol dependence was more prevalent in men with household incomes of less than $25,000.

Alcohol dependence was most common among excessive drinkers: about 10 percent of binge drinkers, but only 1 percent of non-binge drinkers. There was a positive correlation between alcohol dependence and frequent binge drinking. The word *positive* can be confusing in this context. Although the word itself sounds like a good thing, in our context it is not. It simply means that binge drinkers have a much greater chance of becoming alcoholics.

Many people mistakenly believe that all binge drinkers are alcoholics. This is actually not true. While binge drinkers are at higher risk to become dependent on alcohol, about 90 percent of them do not meet the criteria for alcohol dependence, or the newer 2013 diagnostic term *severe alcohol use disorder*. This has significant educational and treatment implications.

The fact that nine out of ten drinkers who binge are not alcoholics is not an endorsement for excessive drinking, but it does mean that we must treat drinkers individually. The old protocol was to send all drinkers experiencing problems to a thirty-day inpatient program and require attendance at twelve-step meetings along with total abstinence from alcohol. This method may actually backfire because the person knows he is not physically dependent on alcohol and is not drinking just to avoid the symptoms of withdrawal. More likely he is partying as opposed to drinking away a feeling. This person will not be able to identify with true alcoholics and may miss the healthy messages about changing drinking patterns. We need, therefore, to tailor treatment to this person's particular needs. Treatment should include helping him understand why he chooses to drink so much, exploring the potential risks of his drinking, and teaching him tools to decrease the amount and frequency of his alcohol consumption. This is exactly what this book is intended to explore.

Call for Change to the Treatment System

Treatment providers need to challenge the mistaken beliefs relating to what actually happens when people drink. Of the people who drink, only a small percentage, about 6 percent of the population, are alcoholics and likely incapable of ever safely drinking again. About one-third of the population drinks socially and never has a problem with their consumption.

There are some drinkers who have experienced consequences to their drinking but might actually be able to continue drinking in a healthier way. They make up about 30 percent of drinkers and could be called problem drinkers. Though their drinking has caused some type of problem for them, it is not severe enough to classify them as alcoholics. This group includes millions of people in the United States alone.

Problem drinkers may be able to reconcile the problems related to their drinking and then drink socially again without losing control. Current treatments have missed the mark on helping this population of drinkers. Some studies have found that after completing an abstinence-only program, only 8 percent of patients remain abstinent from alcohol after 12 weeks. There is something seriously wrong with this number. What other treatment costs $1,000 a day yet boasts less than an 8 percent success rate?

One reason for such a low success rate is the assumption that in order for drinkers to be successful, they must permanently abstain from alcohol. It is wrong to gear all treatment to severe drinkers, especially when they account for only 6 percent of the population. What about the other 94 percent, especially the large group of drinkers who have been experiencing problems related to their drinking? How is it that most programs are still treating all drinkers as alcoholics when they are in fact such a small minority? We need to find alternatives for those drinkers whose consumption has caused a problem but has not ruined their lives or changed their physiology.

Abstinence Is Not the Only Goal

Defining abstinence from alcohol as the primary goal and ultimate measure of success is very limiting. While completely refraining from drinking alcohol is a necessary and life-saving goal for some, many other measures of success also exist. A different way of determining success can be seen in the way I helped a client named Sarah.

Sarah was a twenty-one-year-old college senior who had been charged with two citations for being drunk in public and was on academic suspension for a low grade point average. Some treatment providers would look at her drinking as the problem. However, upon completing a thorough mental-health and substance-use-disorders evaluation, I discovered that Sarah had been sexually assaulted in her freshman year but had never told anyone about it. She was using alcohol to deal with her post-traumatic stress symptoms of insomnia, anxiety, and hypervigilance. Drinking a few beers helped her to fall asleep and not worry about the recurring nightmares of the assault. Taking a few shots before a social gathering helped her forget how anxious she was around the opposite sex, where she now felt all men were predators.

Rather than placing Sarah in the typical mixed-gender education group, I had her participate in several months of individual therapy with me. Our sessions focused on teaching her coping skills to manage the trauma, identifying cognitive distortions, and developing a safety plan. Once these elements were in place, alcohol was no longer a problem for her.

Had Sarah enrolled in a traditional treatment program, she may have been required to attend AA meetings, where she could have become a victim of "thirteenth stepping." This is a practice where some men in AA meetings prey upon vulnerable women and encourage sexual activity as a distraction from alcohol. Additionally, well-intentioned members who mistakenly focused only on her drinking as the problem rather than addressing the trauma she had experienced would have further exacerbated her victim role. This young woman could have walked away with a label that would not have addressed the underlying issues. Instead, through individual therapy she developed other coping skills that dealt with the mental health issues that were causing her to drink.

The Importance of Why

While I typically address how much someone drinks, I have found that it is much more important to explore *why* a person drinks. In that way, I avoid a power struggle and give the client real tools to manage the symptoms and struggles that are contributing to the drinking.

There are many ways to do this, but I usually incorporate some of the following techniques. Psychodynamic therapy helps us understand what alcohol does for you. We then set up a behavior-modification plan. Then we might pull from cognitive behavioral techniques to challenge problematic thoughts and habits. We would then review mindfulness strategies that teach you how to develop skills to manage thoughts and cravings. Using experiential methods, we would then practice using certain skills. This litany demonstrates the many methods that exist to help drinkers get healthier. Treatment is not someone lying on a couch while I ask them how they feel.

To me, it is not important for a person to know the schools of thought for the possible interventions, but it is important that the therapeutic process be specifically tailored to where the person is in the change and recovery process. Additionally, the client must be a willing and invested participant. A therapist should never force his or her beliefs on a client, but rather welcome lively debates. If your therapist has only one way of doing things, it may be time to look for other options.

Why People Avoid Getting Help

Moderation Management (MM) reports that there are four times as many drinkers experiencing problems than alcoholic drinkers. They also note that nine out of ten drinkers will not seek help; that's a whopping 90 percent. MM believes, as do I, that many individuals hold mistaken beliefs about what treatment will require of them. People are concerned that they will be expected to give up drinking completely and will have to attend AA meetings. They also worry that they will never be able to have fun again, that life will be boring, and that they will have to give up all their friends.

The estimate that 90 percent of the people who are having problems with alcohol will not seek help is a very concerning statistic to me. It is sad that so many people will continue suffering because of the mistaken belief that if they are having a problem with drinking, they must be an alcoholic and therefore can never drink again. This is even sadder because the drinker is interconnected with many systems: family members, friends, neighbors, and coworkers. One person with an alcohol problem can literally affect hundreds of people, which in turn affects thousands. In theory, this would mean that every person in the country is either directly or indirectly affected by alcohol.

I do not see how applying what works for only 6 percent of drinkers to all drinkers as an effective treatment strategy. We don't treat everyone who has chest pain as if they were having a heart attack. Doctors examine, order tests, and collect more information before they make a diagnosis and provide treatment. I want you to be an educated consumer of services and find what is right for you.

Doctors also don't perform open-heart surgery on someone who only has heartburn. Similarly, alcohol treatment should be done in the least restrictive environment. Not everyone who drinks too much needs to be in a thirty-day residential program. It is very important to me that all of my clients do something called *self-assessment*. Self-assessment means figuring out the role that alcohol plays in your life and determining a plan of action to deal with it.

Family members who are frustrated with the impact of a loved one's drinking often feel hopeless. Some well-intentioned friends or twelve-step participants may say, "Well, he hasn't hit bottom yet." I believe this is an oversimplification for people who are truly dealing with a substance-use disorder. They may want to make a change but not know how to implement or sustain the change.

When people get sick from diabetes, cancer, or heart disease, we don't necessarily get mad at them. Instead, loved ones may help them change their diet, research treatments for them, or begin an exercise program with them. We don't get angry and leave them to fend for themselves. We work to help them find different ways to cope. The same should be true for people struggling with alcohol problems. I'm not saying to let drinkers off the hook for poor choices. I'm only saying that recovery is complicated and not just a matter of willpower.

Moderate Drinking Research

Studies completed at universities and medical schools around the world have extensively examined moderation strategies. They determined the following:

- Individuals who sought help to moderate their drinking were already experiencing problems related to their consumption but were not physically dependent on alcohol.
- Those who received moderation training were able to reduce their consumption by an average of 50-70 percent, which led

to reduced negative impacts on their health and fewer social problems.

- Positive results were seen not only in drinkers who received professional help, but also in those using a self-help guide.
- Follow-up studies for as long as eight years showed that those who were most successful were the ones who had the least severe problems at the start.
- Those with the most severe problems started with moderation for a period of time but ultimately decided to abstain from alcohol permanently.
- Overall, about one-third of those who initially tried moderation ultimately decided to abstain permanently.

It has been estimated that 75-93 percent of substance-abuse programs require total abstinence from alcohol. Throughout this book, we will address many reasons that warrant periods of alcohol-free time and sometimes complete abstinence. Some of my clients have said that it is actually easier to totally refrain from drinking than to struggle with trying to control their drinking.

In a review of data compiled over four years, SAMHSA discovered that the number one reason that people who needed treatment did not seek it was that they were not ready to stop using substances. Does this mean we just say, "Tough luck; come back when you have hit bottom"? Absolutely not. Providers need to adapt treatment to the client and the problem, not make the person fit into a specific model. We need to take people where they are and provide them with support, education, and tools to help them in their change process. We should never force people into a program that may not even help them. It is our job as clinicians to help figure out, with our clients, the methods and models that might best help them.

In my experience, the best way for me to disarm people is not to square off in front of them and fight back with opinions and knowledge. This will only further distance them from wanting to get help and solidify their belief that professionals don't understand them. I prefer to figuratively walk beside my clients. I want to get to know them and understand their stories, both the good and the bad. In this way, we can figure out together how they arrived at the place where alcohol began causing problems and come up with practical solutions. Clients are more likely to be committed to a favorable outcome when it is their goal, not mine.

Read on to determine whether you can keep drinking.

Harm Reduction

I have found several excellent approaches to helping people with alcohol problems. One of them includes concepts from *harm reduction* models. Harm reduction shifts alcohol abuse from a disease model to a psychosocial model. This means that we get away from the belief that achieving and maintaining abstinence from alcohol is the only way for a person to receive help. Harm reduction explores ways to reduce the harm of the chemical abuse and views small incremental changes as successes. It is better to focus more on what works than to dwell on what doesn't work. The goal is to reduce harm to the drinker and others rather than just holding a person to total abstinence. These models tend to look at the whole person, not just the problem drinking.

Below are the stories of three clients who made small changes and experienced varying rates of success regarding their drinking.

Kate

Kate, a middle-aged mom, used wine to take the edge off her day. She worked full-time and then came home to three kids who had homework to do and practices to get to, and she had to make dinner each night. She felt that a few glasses of wine would make her a better mom because she would not yell as much.

Kate began to recognize that several glasses of wine a night might be a problem when she almost had a car accident coming home from her daughter's dance class. She'd already had four glasses when she suddenly realized that she'd mixed up her carpool dates, but she still hopped into the car to fulfill her driving duties. She almost hurt herself, her daughter, and two of her daughter's friends. Kate was scared, so she called me.

During the initial evaluation, Kate said that after scheduling the appointment with me, she reduced her average intake from six glasses a night to three a night. Rather than launching into a discussion about how bad three drinks were for her, I said, "That's amazing! How did you go from six a day to three? That's like a 50 percent improvement! What did you do to manage the stress of the kids and dinner and work?"

In this way, Kate did not continue to beat herself up. She was able to focus on what was working and develop a plan that focused on building upon her successes rather than punishing her for the mistakes she was already keenly aware of. Kate wanted to come back to therapy because we developed an individualized plan for her that did not focus only on her drinking, but why she was drinking and what we could do about it.

Jackie

Jackie was a binge drinker on the weekends when her kids went to their dad's house. As soon as her ex and his new bimbo pulled out of the driveway, she began sipping a cocktail while getting ready to go out and hit the meat market. Her ex had already found someone, so why shouldn't she? In therapy we worked together to help her deal with the implications of the divorce on her life. She began to value herself again and figure out what she wanted in a relationship instead of just finding someone to fill the hours.

One Friday night Jackie ran up quite a bar tab. The next night she decided to practice some of the skills she was learning in therapy. She checked out the singles group at her friend's synagogue. She had nothing to drink that night and actually enjoyed herself. In our next session, my response was to give her a huge smile, share in her excitement, and process what it was like to have sober conversations where the men were not just looking to hook up.

I focused on the night where she had success rather than on the night where she drank more than what she had planned. I helped her identify other situations where she could socialize with other people in her situation without alcohol. The next weekend that the kids are with their dad, she is planning to go paintballing with some other single parents.

Mike

Mike walked into my office with a sad, guilty look. His shoulders were hunched over, and he could barely look me in the eye. Prior to seeing me, he had gone to detox to break a physical addiction to alcohol and had been told to go to "90 in 90" (ninety AA meetings in ninety days).

Mike hated his job and would often start drinking as soon as he got home from work. In the past, he had often polished off a twelve-pack by the end of the night. Since he got clean, his wife was happy that he had stopped drinking but was frustrated that he was gone every night at an AA meeting. At least when he was drinking, he had been home and could help with the kids a little bit.

Mike remained alcohol free for two months before he couldn't take the stress anymore and went on a bender. He admitted what happened and talked about the huge fight that had ensued with his wife. Together they admitted that they both had issues to work through. They came to the agreement that she would begin working part-time so he could finish his degree and get another job.

Mike expected me to admonish him for the relapse, but I was so excited I could barely contain myself. I congratulated him on working as a team with his wife and coming up with a plan together. I looked at what was important— reconnecting with his best friend, with whom he developed a plan for long-term financial stability and happiness for the whole family—rather than focusing on the one night of drinking that resulted from a poor decision. In fact, this poor decision opened the line of communication that helped this couple regain intimacy and develop a plan to deal with their stressors.

> *Never discourage anyone who continues*
> *to make progress, no matter how slow.*
> —Plato

Moderate Drinking

As you can see in the examples above, alcohol became a problem for each of these people and their families. However, going to a thirty-day inpatient treatment, attending AA meetings, and focusing on total abstinence were not really the main goals. Addressing ways to reduce the harm of drinking and learning to drink in moderation may be a better focus for the more than 90 percent of drinkers who are not physically dependent on alcohol.

An excellent online resource about drinking in moderation is Moderation Management (MM). They have a great website, moderation. org, that offers online support and tools on how to become a successful moderate drinker. MM is a behavioral-change program and national support-group network for people who are concerned about their drinking and have a desire to make positive lifestyle changes. MM empowers individuals to accept personal responsibility for choosing and maintaining their own paths regarding alcohol use. It is the first moderation-based support group to be listed in NIAAA.

The significance of this is that the NIAAA itself has been around only since the 1970s. President Nixon signed the Comprehensive Alcohol Abuse and Alcoholism Prevention, Treatment, and Rehabilitation Act in 1970. It is also known as the Hughes Act, for Senator Harold Hughes, a recovering alcoholic who promoted recovery. Some of you may have been alive when this legislation went into action.

The NIAAA has worked to make alcohol-use disorders recognized more as a medical condition rather than a moral issue. They conduct research that helps us understand the ways alcohol affects us. I mention the Hughes Act because it has been around for only a short period of history, while Alcoholics Anonymous (AA) has been in existence since 1935.

Beyond Alcoholics Anonymous

Bill Wilson and Dr. Bob Smith founded AA during the post-Prohibition era in America when alcoholism was looked at as a moral failure and the medical profession treated it as incurable and lethal. The only requirement to join AA is the desire to stop drinking. One of the primary ways it helps is through self-help groups, but also with sponsorship, fellowship, accountability, and twelve-step work.

In my professional opinion, participation in AA should not be required for everyone who has a problem with drinking. It works for some, but it is not necessary for everyone struggling with alcohol. This opinion is very controversial in my professional field and to the courts that require it as part of probation or parole. Nonetheless, I have found that AA works best for people who are physically and emotionally dependent on alcohol, have few supports, experience regular cravings, and lack structure during the day.

AA is a lifesaver for some people, but because court systems and treatment programs too often require it, AA can actually be a turnoff and prevent people from getting necessary help. I have found that intellectual clients who struggle with a religious or spiritual belief have a very hard time connecting to AA's concept of a higher power and surrendering to it. Additionally, teenagers, women, young adults, and trauma survivors can sometimes be targeted in meetings by those who have not yet addressed their unhealthy behaviors.

I want all people who struggle with alcohol to know that AA is a free resource available anywhere in the world, even on some cruise ships (Friends of Bill). Sometimes, once people are invested in their recovery and the treatment process, they are more open to attending a meeting. For a first meeting, I recommend taking a friend and going to an open meeting or attending a speaker's meeting. These tend to be better for beginners. Participants may feel a little lost if their first time in attendance is at a step meeting, where the focus is on one of the twelve steps, or at a closed meeting, which is only for those in recovery, not friends or family of the alcoholic. If you are considering involvement with AA, try out a few groups; they are as diverse as the people in this country. Go to aa.org for more information about the program and to find a meeting in your area.

Most of us have heard of the twelve steps emphasis of AA. Listed below are the steps.

THE TWELVE STEPS OF ALCOHOLICS ANONYMOUS

1. *We admitted we were powerless over alcohol—that our lives had become unmanageable.*
2. *Came to believe that a Power greater than ourselves could restore us to sanity.*
3. *Made a decision to turn our will and our lives over to the care of God as we understood Him.*
4. *Made a searching and fearless moral inventory of ourselves.*
5. *Admitted to God, to ourselves, and to another human being the exact nature of our wrongs.*
6. *Were entirely ready to have God remove all these defects of character.*

7. *Humbly asked Him to remove our shortcomings.*
8. *Made a list of all persons we had harmed, and became willing to make amends to them all.*
9. *Made direct amends to such people wherever possible, except when to do so would injure them or others.*
10. *Continued to take personal inventory and when we were wrong promptly admitted it.*
11. *Sought through prayer and meditations to improve conscious contact with God as we understood Him, praying only for knowledge of His will for us and the power to carry that out.*
12. *Having had a spiritual awakening as the result of these steps, we try to carry this message to other alcoholics, and to practice these principles in all our affairs.*

Moderate Drinking Defined

Getting back to moderate drinking . . . Again, this is a relatively new and controversial topic. Many traditional therapists, family members, and Alcoholics Anonymous members would argue against me when I suggest moderate drinking for some of those with a drinking problem. But hear me out, and remember the statistics on who is drinking and the small 6 percent who are actually physically dependent on alcohol.

So what is *moderate drinking*? According to the Dietary Guidelines for Americans, moderate drinking is having up to one drink per day for women and up to two drinks per day for men. Let's get real about how much a drink really is: a "40" does not count as one beer, half a bottle of wine poured into a large wineglass is not one drink, and a sixteen-ounce glass filled with bourbon and a splash of soda is not one drink.

What is a standard drink?

The chart below, is really just a guideline; there are many variations. Most American beers contain 5 percent alcohol, but many European, Belgian, Irish, and German beers have much higher alcohol content. So that stout may actually count as two drinks.

Most table wines contain 12 percent alcohol, but this is equal to 3.5 ounces of fortified wine like sherry or port. A mere 2.5 ounces of a cordial contain 24 percent alcohol—that's why such a small glass is used.

Usually, 1.5 ounces of liquor like gin, rum, vodka, or whiskey is 80-proof. Watch out for liquors that can go as high as 151- to even 190-proof. Be especially aware of grain alcohol or moonshine. Just like you should have an idea of the number of calories in the food you consume, you should be aware of the proof of the liquor you drink. All drinks are not necessarily equal in the impact they have. As noted previously, the impact of taking a shot is different from sipping a mixed drink. Alcohol also affects you differently depending on whether you are drinking while eating or on an empty stomach.

At this point, you still do not know whether you can continue drinking at your present amount and frequency, whether you should

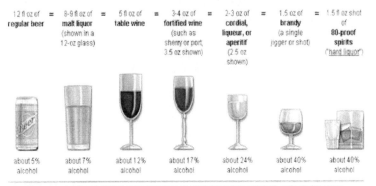

| 12 fl oz of regular beer | = | 8-9 fl oz of malt liquor (shown in a 12-oz glass) | = | 5 fl oz of table wine | = | 3-4 oz of fortified wine (such as sherry or port, 3.5 oz shown) | = | 2-3 oz of cordial, liqueur, or aperitif (2.5 oz shown) | = | 1.5 oz of brandy (a single jigger or shot) | = | 1.5 fl oz shot of 80-proof spirits ("hard liquor") |
| about 5% alcohol | | about 7% alcohol | | about 12% alcohol | | about 17% alcohol | | about 24% alcohol | | about 40% alcohol | | about 40% alcohol |

The percent of "pure" alcohol, expressed here as alcohol by volume (alc/vol), varies by beverage cut down, or whether it is crucial to your health for you to eliminate alcohol from your life. The next chapter will give you an opportunity to self-assess and explore the cost/benefit paradigm of drinking.

INTERESTING INFO: Why can men drink more than women? Why are they allowed two drinks a day and women get only one? Alcohol is typically dispersed through the body in water, and women, because they generally weigh less than men, have less water in their bodies. Therefore, women will have a higher concentration of alcohol in their bodies than do men.

Women also often become more intoxicated than men with an equivalent amount of alcohol. This is partly because of a difference in the activity of an enzyme in the stomach tissue of males and females that breaks alcohol down before it reaches the bloodstream. The enzyme is four times more active in males than in females. Also, women proportionately have more body fat than males and less body water than males. Because alcohol is more soluble in water than in fat, the amount of alcohol becomes more highly concentrated in a female's body than in a male's. Additionally, as the proportion of body fat increases with age, it is recommended that older adults limit their consumption to one drink per day.

ANOTHER ROUND OF CHAPTER 2
Why Are All Alcohol Users Treated the Same?

- About 30 percent of alcohol users are considered problem drinkers.
- Only 6 percent of drinkers are considered severe drinkers, or alcoholics.
- The majority of treatment facilities define complete abstinence as success.
- Twelve-step groups should not be required for all drinkers with problems.
- Moderation Management is an excellent online tool to assist in moderate drinking.
- Harm reduction models view incremental changes as success.
- Moderate drinking is no more than two drinks a day for men and one drink a day for women.

Chapter 3

Self-Assessment

efore trying to figure out whether you can keep drinking, you have to figure out if you have a problem. So what is normal drinking? A simple way I define it is: "the way a majority of people would think or act in a given situation." In other words, if a hundred people were in a room, at least fifty-one of them would respond similarly in a given situation.

If more than half of all adults drink alcohol, but only 6 percent meet the criteria for a severe alcohol-use disorder, why is drinking such a big deal? Remember, it is usually only this 6 percent group that can never safely drink again. You, as an individual, must look at how drinking alcohol affects your life. The drinking habits of your twenties may differ from the drinking habits of your thirties, once you have a career, mortgage, kids, and other responsibilities to consider. The drinking patterns of your thirties and forties may not cause problems then, but as you grow older, you may begin to drink more in an attempt to get the same effect you enjoyed previously. Or maybe your increased drinking stems from the fact that your significant other kicked you out of the bed because you snore too much, you no longer have sex, and your doctor is on you about your weight, cholesterol, and blood pressure.

Functioning Alcoholic?

Once when I was testifying as an expert witness, the judge asked me to define the term *functioning alcoholic.* The question she posed actually required a rather lengthy answer. I was on the stand for almost an hour as I explained that it depends on what one considers to be "functioning," and that the definition of *alcoholic* is not actually a clinical term and should not be tossed around lightly.

Is a functioning alcoholic someone with a college degree who is holding down a minimum-wage job? Is it staying married but passing out on the couch every night? Is it the wife who still maintains custody of her kids, but the television babysits them while she sneaks wine in the laundry room? Is the college student who takes seven years to graduate a functioning alcoholic? I know I don't want to be any of them, regardless of whether or not they qualify as functioning alcoholics.

I think the term *functioning alcoholic* is very misleading. It is actually very rare that a drinker is so far gone that he has lost his freedom, health, job, house, kids, and spouse. The stereotype of an alcoholic is someone who is homeless and drinks out of a brown paper bag under a bridge, but this is not accurate. Many people with a drinking problem are still able to function in their activities and roles of daily living but are underachieving and often suffering from a great deal of emotional pain.

When evaluating your drinking, you may have done what I call "comparing out." This means looking at exceptions to validate continued use. You may want to believe that you don't have a problem because you have not lost everything. You may think you couldn't possibly have a problem because you still hold down a job, have earned a degree, maintain a close, intimate relationship, or have not experienced any legal or medical complications from drinking.

I think it is important to examine the quality of these areas of life. They don't have to be lost for your drinking to be a problem. They just have to be impacted in some negative way. You may not think you have a problem, but your boss, spouse, friends, teachers, probation officer, or doctor may feel otherwise.

INTERESTING INFO: The words *alcoholic* and *alcoholism* were coined in 1848 by a Swedish physician named Magnus Huss. By the end of the twentieth century it had become the accepted way of describing alcohol problems, particularly in the United States where people with drinking problems were previously called drunkards or inebriates.

DSM-5 Diagnosis

Believe it or not, *alcoholic* is not actually a clinical term. It's just a name that people use for heavy drinkers. The way that professionals make a clinical diagnosis is with the *Diagnostic and Statistical Manual*, 5th edition (DSM-5). This is the book that clinicians, including doctors, psychiatrists, social workers, therapists, and psychologists, use to diagnose emotional and behavioral problems. Insurance companies require a DSM diagnosis to provide reimbursement for behavioral health services.

The DSM-5 came out in May 2013. One of its major changes is in the way clinicians diagnose substance-use disorders. Formerly, only two categories for alcohol misuse existed: abuse or dependence. I described them as:

Alcohol abuse: If alcohol use causes a problem, it is a problem.

Alcohol dependence: This term describes a person needing to drink to avoid physical withdrawal symptoms and needing more and more of it to achieve the same effect. This is the person we call an alcoholic.

Many people incorrectly interchanged the two definitions. This was dangerous because the two alcohol categories are very different. It is important to note that someone who is physically dependent on alcohol is unlikely to ever be able to safely drink again; but the much larger group of alcohol abusers, with the right tools and supports, may be able to safely drink again.

The DSM-5 eliminated the category of dependence to help distinguish between the compulsive drug-seeking behavior of addiction and the normal tolerance and withdrawal that patients who are legally prescribed medication may experience when stopping their prescriptions. The diagnoses were also recategorized on a continuum to include mild, moderate, and severe substance-use disorders. The information below is taken directly from the DSM-5.

As you are reading, check off the ones that apply to you.

Alcohol Use Disorder:

A. A problematic pattern of alcohol use leading to clinically significant impairment or distress, as manifested by at least two of the following, occurring within a 12-month period:

☐ Alcohol is often taken in larger amounts or over a longer period than was intended.

☐ There is a persistent desire or unsuccessful efforts to cut down or control alcohol use.

☐ A great deal of time is spent in activities necessary to obtain alcohol, use alcohol, or recover from its effects.

☐ Craving, or a strong desire or urge to use alcohol.

☐ Recurrent alcohol use resulting in a failure to fulfill major role obligations at work, school, or home.

☐ Continued alcohol use despite having persistent or recurrent social or interpersonal problems caused or exacerbated by the effect of alcohol.

☐ Important social, occupational, or recreational activities are given up or reduced because of alcohol use.

☐ Recurrent alcohol use in situations in which it is physically hazardous.

☐ Alcohol use is continued despite knowledge of having a persistent or recurrent physical problem that is likely to be exacerbated by alcohol.

☐ Tolerance, as defined by either of the following:

    a. A need for markedly increased amounts of alcohol to achieve intoxication or desired effect.

    b. A markedly diminished effect with continued use of the same amount of alcohol.

☐ Withdrawal, as manifested by either of the following:

    a. The characteristic withdrawal syndrome for alcohol (see below)

    b. Alcohol (or a closely related substance, such as a benzodiazepine) is taken to relieve or avoid withdrawal symptoms

The DSM-5 now looks at chemical use on a continuum similar to the spectrum of alcohol use described in chapter 2:

Mild Alcohol Use Disorder: presence of two to three symptoms
Moderate Alcohol Use Disorder: presence of four to five symptoms
Severe Alcohol Use Disorder: presence of six or more symptoms

How many of these symptoms have you experienced? Was it in the past, or is it in the present? Obviously, the fewer symptoms you have experienced, the more likely you are to be successful in attempting to moderate your drinking.

Alcohol Withdrawal

Because I believe it is important for people to have accurate information, I have also included the criteria for alcohol withdrawal. Many people are confused about the difference between a hangover—which may include gastric distress, grogginess, nausea, vomiting, and headache—and true alcohol withdrawal. Since experiencing actual alcohol withdrawal can be potentially life threatening, it is important to determine whether you have had just one too many or are actually experiencing a dangerous medical condition. Continue reading to help identify the difference.

Alcohol Withdrawal

A. Cessation of (or reduction in) alcohol use that has been heavy and prolonged

B. Two (or more) of the following, developing within several hours to a few days after the cessation of (or reduction in) alcohol use as described in criterion A:

1. Autonomic hyperactivity (e.g. sweating or pulse rate greater than 100 bpm)
2. Increased hand tremor
3. Insomnia

4. Nausea or vomiting
5. Transient, visual, tactile, or auditory hallucinations or illusions
6. Psychomotor agitation
7. Anxiety
8. Generalized tonic-clonic seizures (formerly known as gran mal seizures)

C. The signs or symptoms in criterion B cause clinically significant distress or impairment in social, occupational, or other important areas of functioning.

D. The signs or symptoms are not attributable to another medical condition and are not better explained by another mental disorder, including intoxication or withdrawal from another substance.

How many of these symptoms have you experienced? Please realize that if you have had any of them, it is highly unlikely that you will be able to safely drink again. As one of my clients once said in group, "It's like being a pickle. You start out as a cucumber, but once you reach a certain point in your drinking, you turn into a pickle. And you can't go back to being a cucumber, no matter how bad you want it." Most doctors recommend that if you have seizures, fever, hallucinations, or delirium tremens (the "shakes"), you need to go to your nearest emergency room or call 911.

Experiencing delirium tremens, or the shakes, is very dangerous. Alcohol often initially enhances the effect of GABA (gamma-aminobutyric acid), a neurotransmitter that produces feelings of relaxation and calm and can also induce sleep. However, heavy use of alcohol suppresses GABA so that the body requires more and more of it to achieve the same effect, a condition otherwise known as tolerance. Heavy alcohol use also suppresses glutamate, the neurotransmitter that produces excitability. When regular users stop drinking, the chemicals rebound and can cause dangerous consequences such as seizures.

I have seen both men and women go through withdrawal from drinking all types of alcohol, including beer, wine, and liquor. This medical condition does not distinguish between users. Potentially life-threatening withdrawal symptoms can begin as early as two hours after the last drink, but the dangerous symptoms often begin to peak around forty-eight to seventy-two hours after alcohol cessation. Delirium tremens, however, may not peak until five days after stopping drinking. A person with the shakes needs to get medical attention immediately because it can progress to life-threateningly high blood pressure.

If you are a heavy daily drinker who wants to cut down or stop drinking, you should talk with a medical professional to see how to do this safely. At this point, your treatment will focus on medically managing the symptoms of withdrawal, not addressing the underlying reasons for your drinking or the ways to manage long-term recovery. Many people mistakenly believe that once they complete the three to seven days of a hospital detox, they are finished with treatment and will be fine. This, however, is only the first step. It's like going to the hospital for back surgery. Your medical issue may be addressed, but once you return home, you must undergo physical therapy and implement appropriate lifestyle changes to prevent reinjury. In chapter 10, I will review treatment options for those who do not think they can safely moderate their drinking.

Cost/Benefit Analysis

One of the steps that I recommend early in treatment is for clients to perform a cost/benefit analysis of alcohol use.

Cost/Benefit of Drinking Paradigm

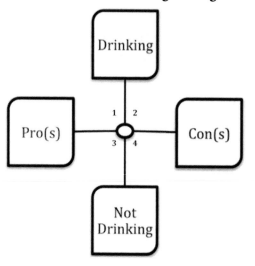

Much of traditional therapy focuses on quadrants 2 and 3, the consequences of drinking and the benefits of not drinking. In fact, during the first few days of a traditional thirty-day rehabilitation program, for several of the nine hours of an IOP (intensive outpatient program), and in many sessions of court-ordered groups, the focus is on the impact of alcohol use. Much of the information has been provided in a "scared straight" manner. However, studies have shown that this type of education does not yield an effective long-term impact. Not understanding this reality, parents, friends, and family members of problem drinkers tend to dwell on the idea that if their loved ones knew what they were doing to themselves, they would surely stop. You and I know that addiction and problem drinking do not work this way.

Quadrant 2 explores the cons of drinking. Almost everyone has some idea of the negative impacts of drinking. I'm sure you can list numerous legal, health, relational, and mood problems. I have found that although people can usually identify these negative consequences, it is often in a general, impersonal way. If time in treatment is dedicated to education, I believe it should be personalized to what you are actually or potentially experiencing. All too often, however, professionals and family members focus on scare tactics. For many, scare tactics simply cause them to tune out the message, and the extreme examples make them further feel like "that could never happen to me." Quadrant 3 is very similar to the second quadrant in that it is very logical. Most people can identify why it would be good to stop drinking. I have found that the most effective therapy occurs and real change takes place when we explore the first and fourth quadrants. This should be personalized and individualized to the problems that personally affect the one struggling with drinking.

It is crucial for those trying to help problem drinkers to identify and acknowledge the benefits of drinking. Obviously, you would not have continued to drink if it were all bad. The severe consequences often do not begin until years into the established drinking patterns. Exploring the benefits of drinking accomplishes several things for drinkers experiencing problems. Hopefully, it puts you at ease, reducing your defensiveness and validating that you are not crazy or being judged for engaging in the drinking behavior. Second, helping you identify why you drink allows you to devise a plan of action. Third, it begins the process of grieving the death of old drinking patterns and establishing a healthier relationship with alcohol.

Donna was a forty-five-year-old mother of three kids. From the outside, she looked like the ideal stay-at-home mom. She made the kids' lunches every day, always volunteered in their classrooms, drove the carpools, and could be counted on if anyone needed a favor.

What none of the people who admired her knew was that Donna suffered from low self-esteem, depression, and anxiety. She believed that if she could make everything look fine, it would be fine. No one knew that once she dropped off the kids, she began sipping vodka throughout the day to get rid of her fears and negative emotions. By the time her husband and kids got home, she was quite buzzed but forced herself to make a dinner from scratch, do crafts for the Girl and Boy Scout troops, and bake for the church fundraiser.

One morning her husband took out the recycling and was shocked to see the empty vodka bottles in the bin. His first thought was that his wife must have been having an affair with a man who drank a lot. There was no way his perfect wife could have a drinking problem. Her husband confronted her, and she tearfully admitted how stressed out, sad, and anxious she really was.

Donna began treatment. While she was away in the rehabilitation center, the family had to figure out ways to manage all of the responsibilities that Donna had taken on and overachieved in. In treatment, Donna learned that she had value for who she was, not what she did. She practiced setting limits, using positive self-talk, and implementing more effective coping skills.

Donna and her family are much happier these days. The family now spends time doing the activities that they enjoy, and Donna finds fulfillment in these, rather than by checking off items she thought were expected of her. The kids had always wondered why Mommy's smile did not reach her eyes, but now they play games and have tickle fights instead of running to the next activity.

The fourth quadrant offers another perspective in exploring the benefits derived from drinking. In preparing to make a change, all involved have to look at what happens if a person does decide to stop drinking or attempts to moderate drinking.

Pat and Bill were high school sweethearts. They had been married for over twenty years. Drinking was a part of the way they socialized, relaxed, celebrated, and vacationed. They enjoyed going to wine tastings and beer festivals. The couple also enjoyed cooking and figuring out which wines paired best with their meals. If they were stressed out or angry with each other, they just had a drink. In this way, they were able to avoid many fights. But they eventually discovered that more and more resentments were not getting addressed because they were ignoring the problems and just getting buzzed.

One night on the way home from a get-together with friends, Bill was pulled over for a DUI infraction. Both he and Pat had consumed a number of drinks, but neither felt intoxicated. After years of drinking, their tolerance level had become quite high.

Bill hired an attorney for court but still had to serve ten days in jail for a high Breathalyzer reading. Additionally, he was required to have an interlock system installed on his car (an apparatus that he had to blow into and be alcohol free to start his car) and complete sixteen weeks of an education class while remaining alcohol free. During this time, Pat and Bill were forced to examine how much drinking had become a part of their relationship and to come up with better communication strategies, because life was not always a party.

Pat realized that she could not blame Bill for the DUI because she'd had just as much to drink as he did. Deep down, she knew she had to change too.

Despite their poor method of communication, they loved each other very much and decided to reevaluate the ways they could spend their free time together and resolve problems. They signed up for a dance class, started hiking, and focused more time on activities than on alcohol. Pat and Bill participated in a couples' retreat with their church and learned how to communicate with each other directly rather than trying to drink issues away.

Even though the restrictions that the court imposed on Bill have now been satisfied, the couple no longer makes alcohol a priority. By having drinks only on special occasions rather than every night, they have both lost weight, enjoy more energy, and deal with issues as they arise. Instead of sipping mixed drinks on the beach for their next vacation, they are planning a high adventure trip where they will kayak, rock climb, and zip line. People who know them say they look and act ten years younger.

Moderation Resources

I encourage you to explore the resources that support the reality that not all drinkers are alcoholics but still may need some help.

Hamsnetwork.org (harm reduction, abstinence, and moderation support) lists treatment providers who support safer or reduced drinking and also offers online forums, chat groups, written materials, podcasts, and live meetings.

Moderation.org (Moderation Management) provides listings of moderation-friendly therapists, online forums, chat groups, and face-to-face meetings for those considering moderation.

Psychologytoday.com has a find-a-therapist link where interested parties can read about providers' specialties and look at their biographies before making an appointment with someone in their area.

Smartrecovery.org (self-management and recovery training) lists people who have completed thirty hours of training on SMART recovery principles, offers online resources, maintains lists of local meetings, and sponsors an online community. SMART promotes abstinence but allows people attempting moderation to attend.

If you have a problem with drinking, there is help for you. But you will have to be brave, take a risk, and see what a person or program has to offer. If you don't find the right fit on your first try, don't give up. Look for someone or something else that works better for you. Remember that your problems did not develop overnight, and it will take time for change to occur and for you to experience some relief. The more time and effort that you put into healthier choices, the more benefits you will experience.

ANOTHER ROUND OF CHAPTER 3
Self-Assessment

- Before figuring out if you can keep drinking, explore the role that alcohol plays in your life.
- The DSM-5 looks at substance-use disorders on a continuum. The more symptoms you experience, the less likelihood that you can drink moderately.
- If you have experienced tolerance to or withdrawal symptoms from alcohol, you may not be a good candidate for moderate drinking.
- Alcohol withdrawal can be life-threatening. If you are experiencing withdrawal symptoms, you should seek immediate medical attention.
- The cost/benefit paradigm of drinking encourages you to focus less on the reasons to stop drinking and the harm of continuing use, and more on the benefits derived from alcohol use.
- Understanding the benefits of drinking and the cons to stopping alcohol use allows you to come up with a plan of action that will be more effective in making a long-term change to the current pattern.
- Check out the multiple online and in-person resources that are available for people who are considering moderate drinking.

INTERESTING INFO: Did you know that there is a way to test for alcohol use from three to four days prior? A Breathalyzer, urine screen, or blood test measures how much alcohol is in your system. There is a new test, however, that measures the amount of ethyl glucuronide (ETG) in your system. ETG is a direct metabolite of the alcohol that you drink and remains in the body even after the alcohol itself can no longer be detected. The presence of ETG in urine indicates recent alcohol consumption, often up to eighty hours, even though the alcohol may no longer be in your system.

Chapter 4

What Does Alcohol Do To Our Bodies?

lcohol affects every organ in the body, including the brain. The life expectancy of someone who drinks heavily is shorter than that of others who drink less. Approximately 40 percent of all hospital beds in the United States (excluding maternity and intensive care patients) are used to treat health conditions related to alcohol consumption.

I want to give you some information that you may not want to hear. I'm not trying to preach, but I believe that you need to realize the impact of the alcohol you consume and understand the way it affects your brain and body. I will also discuss the other ways drinking affects you—that is, its impact on the activities of daily living that involve the people, goals, and responsibilities that are important to you. Listed below are the typical activities for each of the various age groups.

For adolescents, this might include learning in school, playing sports or music, exploring social relationships, and developing emotional, familial, and social coping skills.

For young adults, earning a degree or job skill, finding a job, developing romantic relationships, and establishing independence are important activities.

Adults are typically engaged in advancing their careers, caring for their children or aging parents, maintaining a home, paying a mortgage, and achieving deeper intimacy in relationships.

Older adults are beginning retirement, enjoying relationships with their grown children and grandchildren, and interested in maintaining health.

Drinking can impact any of these age groups and their day-to-day activities, goals, and skills.

Damage from alcohol is seen not only in our bodies, but also in our moods and decision-making abilities. One-third of the deaths related to alcohol abuse come from suicides, accidents, and drowning. To put this in perspective, approximately thirty people die every day from an alcohol-related incident.

I believe that all of us are entitled to unbiased information about what we put into our bodies and the impact it has on us. Below I have compiled some of the main effects of alcohol. The impact that drinking has on you individually depends on many factors, including your age, weight, other co-occurring mental or physical health disorders, how much and how often you drink, your gender, the presence of other foods or drugs in your system, and the time period in which the alcohol is consumed. Bear with me…

Central Nervous System

To start, alcohol is a central nervous system depressant. Depressants are a class of drugs that slow down the functioning of the brain by depressing the central nervous system (CNS). What is the CNS? This system of the body includes the brain and the spinal cord. The CNS controls most of our main functions: taking in information, controlling motor function, thinking, understanding, reasoning, and emoting. Not to get overly technical, but the CNS also deals with neurons that form a network that carries information to and from our extremities, muscles, and organs. When the CNS is working properly, the neurons can send signals to and from the brain at speeds up to two hundred miles per hour.

Alcohol is one of the most popular depressants. We often use it to unwind and relax. The calming effects of depressants can be pleasurable. Initially, we may feel more energized as the alcohol reduces inhibitions and helps us be more sociable. This is why alcohol is often called a "social lubricant." Alcohol also helps us to temporarily forget our problems. This all sounds really great, but what happens to the brain and body when we drink too much or too often?

Chronic, Progressive, Fatal

When people talk about alcoholism as a disease that is "chronic, progressive, and fatal," they are serious. Alcohol is the third-largest contributor to disease in the world. It is even worse than nicotine (cigarette) use. Approximately eighty thousand deaths occur each year related to alcohol problems that could have been prevented. Alcoholism is a slow, chronic disease, whereas binge drinking causes many accidents. Generally, the more and the longer you drink, the more damage to your brain and body.

In my practice, the clients who develop cancer, have cirrhosis, need a liver transplant, and suffer from alcohol-induced dementia tend to be chronic, heavy drinkers. However, there are exceptions where I have seen these problems in people as young as in their twenties and thirties. I want you to be the positive exception, not the one whose problems could have been prevented.

Brain

The effect of alcohol on the brain is very concerning. Alcohol interferes with the brain's communication pathways. Drinking alcohol can cause changes in mood and behavior as well as make it difficult to process information and think clearly. It also affects coordination. Functional MRIs show that the regions of the brain most affected by alcohol are the cerebellum, limbic system, and cerebral cortex.

The cerebellum, located in the back of the brain, is the area that controls motor coordination. In the short term, damage to the cerebellum includes a loss of balance and resultant stumbling. Alcohol use also affects memory and emotional responses. People under the influence tend to have more injuries and lapses in judgment. These are the main reasons why alcohol impairs the ability to operate a motor vehicle. People who are intoxicated tend to have accidents because of damage to the cerebellum.

The limbic system is responsible for memory and emotions. Have you ever noticed that you forget some of the things you did when you were drunk? You may have done or said things that were out of character for you because your inhibitions were lowered, but you may not remember doing or saying them. Have you ever noticed how some people always seem to end up in a fight when they are drunk, or some women always seem to end up sobbing about some relatively minor event? This is the alcohol messing with their emotions. We loosen up with one or two drinks, but an excess of alcohol alters our feelings and perceptions of what is being said or done around us.

The cerebral cortex regulates our ability to think, plan, and behave intelligently, and it connects to the rest of the nervous system. Damage to it affects the ability to solve problems, remember, and learn. Have you ever been drinking and come up with the most amazing plan, only to wake up the next morning and wonder why you thought the idea was so great only a few hours ago? Have you ever watched a video of yourself singing or dancing when you were intoxicated? Last night you were amazing, but in the light of day . . . I won't remind you now that your brain is functioning again.

Alcohol affects the neurotransmitters in the brain. These include serotonin, endorphins, and glutamine. You may have heard of serotonin in connection with antidepressants. A certain class of medication prescribed to help with depression is called SSRIs (selective serotonin reuptake inhibitors). Serotonin helps regulate emotional expression. People who suffer from depression are thought to have problems with the levels of serotonin in their brains. Alcohol is believed to deplete the availability of serotonin; thus people who are regular drinkers may suffer from higher rates of depression than those who do not partake.

Endorphins are another type of neurotransmitter that alcohol interferes with. Endorphins are natural substances that increase feelings of relaxation and euphoria. Again, when we drink we feel good initially, but over time these important chemicals are damaged. It makes it harder for natural events and experiences to bring genuine happiness and feelings of pleasure.

The third main neurotransmitter that alcohol damages is glutamine. It is believed that glutamine is responsible for memory. Even moderate drinking can cause people to have fuzzy memories. Think back to the fights you may have had with your loved ones about something you agreed to do while you were drinking or something you said while drinking but now have limited recall of. Damage to glutamine production may contribute to why people who drink heavily black out.

A neuropsychologist with whom I consult has said many times that alcohol is a neurotoxin. Alcohol literally causes brain damage, while long-term drinking actually shrinks the brain. Alcohol alters neurons, which reduces the size of brain cells. The brain mass shrinks and the inner cavity grows bigger.

These changes in the brain affect a wide variety of abilities, including motor coordination, sleep, mood, learning, and memory. As you read through this chapter, I hope that you are mentally doing a cost/benefit analysis. Think about why, despite the real structural, chemical, emotional, and physical damage that regular drinking can do, you want to continue using alcohol at a level that may negatively affect your health and quality of life.

Cardiovascular System

Still with me?

Another significant area that alcohol impacts is the cardiovascular system, which consists of the heart, blood vessels, and blood. The cardiovascular system is working every second of the day, delivering oxygen and nutrients to the cells and carrying away unnecessary materials.

The heart is the center of the cardiovascular system. Chronic drinking causes the heart to experience a wide variety of complications. The heart may develop cardiomyopathy, a stretching and drooping of the heart muscle, which weakens the heart and prevents it from pumping enough blood to nourish the organs. Another complication of the heart is atrial fibrillation, an arrhythmia in which the upper chambers of the heart do not contract properly. This can lead to a blood clot or stroke. Alcohol use also exacerbates the various problems that lead to strokes, hypertension, arrhythmias, and cardiomyopathy.

Additionally, the lifestyle of regular alcohol users contributes to health problems. Drinkers often stay up late, smoke cigarettes, use other drugs, and may not eat healthfully or exercise regularly.

Liver and Pancreas

One organ we may not think a lot about is the liver. The liver's job is to detoxify, synthesize protein, and produce chemicals necessary for digestion. Heavy drinking can cause inflammation, which leads to stenosis (a fatty liver); alcoholic hepatitis (inflammation); fibrosis, a change in the liver caused by inflammation; and cirrhosis, complication of liver disease which involves loss of liver cells and irreversible scarring of the liver. All of these can be fatal. When the liver is damaged, it can no longer function well and allows toxic substances to travel to the brain.

The pancreas is another organ that does not get a lot of attention until it is too late. Alcohol causes the pancreas to produce toxic substances that can lead to pancreatitis, a dangerous inflammation and swelling of the blood vessels that prevents proper digestion. Sitting in a room with alcohol users suffering from liver or pancreas damage is heartbreaking. Often it is only after the damage is so far gone and the person is suffering serious medical complications that he decides it is time to make a change. Sadly, it is often too late at this point.

Liver failure is a horrible way to die. When the body can no longer process toxins, the result is painful and debilitating. The person may become sick and bloated and lose his mind. People who love this person suffer deeply as well. Unfortunately, the damage was preventable, but the only cure now is a liver transplant.

If you are a regular drinker, please see your doctor and ask to have your liver enzymes checked. If they are elevated, you may need to make some significant lifestyle changes before it is too late.

Immune System

Drinking too much or too often can increase the risk of developing certain cancers, including mouth, esophageal, throat, liver, and breast cancer. Alcohol weakens the immune system, making us more susceptible to diseases and sicknesses. Drinking slows the body's ability to fight off infections for twenty-four hours after consumption. Not to be gross, but think about how often you have to go to the bathroom when you are drinking. Where do you go, and do you care at that point about washing your hands?

Pregnancy

For women or people whose partners are pregnant, *fetal alcohol syndrome* (FAS) has horrible consequences on a developing baby. If a woman consumes alcohol while pregnant, she exposes her baby to this risk. Symptoms in a baby with FAS include abnormal facial features and severe reductions in brain function and overall growth. The child's brain will be smaller than normal and have fewer brain cells. This child will have lifelong learning and behavioral problems that will likely decrease his or her quality of life. FAS is the leading preventable birth defect in the United States.

Driving

The Centers for Disease Control and Prevention report that there are 88,000 alcohol-related deaths per year. The National Highway Traffic Safety Administration estimates that of the 32,719 people who died in traffic crashes in 2013 in the United States, 10,076 died in drunk-driving crashes. Alcohol was the reason for one-third of those deaths. Mothers Against Drunk Driving (MADD) reports that every two minutes someone in the United States is injured in an alcohol-related accident and that drunk driving costs the United States $200 billion a year.

I'm going to get on my soapbox here. These are very preventable statistics. If you have consumed more than one drink, do not drive a car. If you need help, get it. If a loved one is suffering from the consequences of alcohol use, talk to someone about how to get help for him or her. If you are the one with a drinking problem, know that many different types of treatment are available. Do something! Okay, I'm done.

If you are reading this book, you are probably willing to address your use of alcohol, or perhaps you want to help someone who is struggling. Thank you for sticking with me so far. I truly believe we all should be educated consumers about what we put into our bodies and the effects it can have on us and the people around us. Humans are social creatures, and no matter how alone we may feel at times, we are all interconnected. The information I just presented is frightening if you are dealing with alcohol misuse personally, but it is also painful for the people in your life. They may be watching you suffer from these consequences and feel hopeless and helpless about what to do.

Donuts?

Remember, drinking alcohol is like eating donuts. Having one or two occasionally isn't going to hurt you, but having a few every day is going to have serious consequences to your health.

INTERESTING INFO: The doctor did not give you all the information. An occasional glass of red wine does have some health benefits. One benefit is the relaxation that sipping a glass of wine can bring. However, it is actually the flavonoids and resveratrol that make wine healthy for us.

More than one glass of wine negates the health benefits and starts becoming harmful. Did you know that you could get the same benefit from eating grapes or taking in healthy fiber? There are supplements available too, and without the calories found in wine. One drink of wine may offer some heart-health benefits, but two drinks erase those effects. It's better to hit the gym than the bottle!

Red wine may also boost levels of HDL, the good cholesterol. Having more HDL cholesterol can help remove LDL, the bad cholesterol, possibly reducing the risk of blood clots. Nonetheless, the American Heart Association recommends against starting drinking, as there are other, healthier ways to prevent heart disease.

ANOTHER ROUND OF CHAPTER 4
What Does Alcohol Do to Our Bodies?

- Alcohol affects every organ in the body, including the brain.
- Drinking can cause a dangerous depression of the central nervous system, where alcohol withdrawal can be life-threatening.
- Alcohol affects balance, memory, sleep, coordination, emotions, and judgment.
- Regular drinking negatively impacts the ability to experience pleasure, resulting in higher rates of depression for drinkers.
- Chronic drinking causes severe damage to the cardiovascular system, elevating the risk for heart attacks, strokes, and blood clots.
- Alcohol depresses the immune system, making us more likely to get sick and be susceptible to diseases.
- Drinking is responsible for over one-third of driving deaths.
- You have the ability to prevent all of these problems!

Chapter 5

Are You Ready To Make A Change?

Are you ready to make some changes to your drinking patterns? The following Stages of Change model can be very helpful in determining where you are with your mental and physical readiness to address your concerns about alcohol. You need to know where you are before you can move forward. Once you figure this out, you will have a better idea of where to start and whether you are actually ready to make any changes.

James Prochaska and Carlo DiClemente developed this model in the late 1970s. They were actually studying how smokers were able to give up their habit, but it applies just as well to the evaluation of alcohol use. They identified five changes and the corresponding actions.

Stages of Change

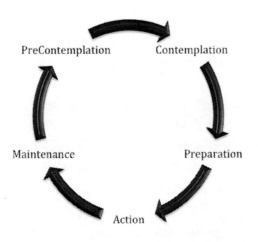

PreContemplation   Contemplation

Maintenance   Preparation

Action

Precontemplation

If you are in the precontemplation stage, you may not consider your alcohol use a problem. You may not yet have experienced any negative consequences, or you may not be ready to acknowledge the severity of consequences that have already occurred. You are not ready to acknowledge that there is a problem behavior that needs to change.

Mark was a twenty-two-year-old college senior who was treasurer of his fraternity. To him this basically meant that he kept track of the keg money and ordered the beer for the weekend parties. Mark was proud that he could drink more than all of his fraternity brothers. He often went out during the week too, because he was a senior and wanted to have fun before joining the real world.

One night Mark was pulled over and given a DUI citation. He spent the night in jail, lost his driver's license, and was ordered to complete sixteen weeks of substance-use education. Mark was furious. He thought that he was just like his frat brothers, and after four years of hard work, he felt he had the right to have a little fun. Mark compared himself with his friends and did not think he was any worse than they were. He had only wanted to get home from the bar that night, and he felt that the cops in his area were just out to make money on the fines. They should be arresting the real criminals, he thought. Mark was not yet ready to make any changes.

How do you work with someone in the precontemplation stage? In our example above, Mark is not thinking of making any changes in his life at this time. He does not acknowledge that there could be a problem. Up until the DUI, his drinking had been fun and he had experienced few consequences, most likely because he was responsible only for himself.

For Mark to get the most out of the court-ordered education, his group leader must validate that he is not yet ready to make a change. Trust must be established, because Mark is an unwilling participant. Friends or family members who are concerned about him can also express concern and point out how they have been affected by his drinking; however, they all should clarify that any decision to change is his. The goal in the precontemplation stage is to explore the impact of Mark's drinking, not to force him to make changes to his drinking. Emphasis should be on what the people in his life, especially romantic partners, say about his use, the way his choices might affect his job search, and whether his ability to be independent is compromised by his drinking.

At this stage, forcing people to do something against their will often backfires because they may not acknowledge that they have a problem. They will often fight back and become more entrenched in their belief that they are just like everyone else. In my work, I try to make the exploration nonjudgmental yet personal. I often include examples of people with whom they can identify and share how these people dealt with their issues.

Sometimes more negative consequences occur, and the expanded thought process can push a person into the next stage.

Contemplation

If you are in the contemplation stage, you are probably beginning to acknowledge a problem with your drinking, and you may be thinking about taking steps to make a change. Although you may have tried to cut down or modify your drinking patterns, you may not yet be ready to make substantial changes.

Lauren was a thirty-year-old single professional. As part of her job, she attended quite a few marketing events, which were often held in bars or restaurants. Initially, Lauren was very nervous with the social aspect of her job and uncomfortable with the idea of trying to sell herself to get new business. When she first started, she would have a glass of wine or two to help her loosen up and feel more comfortable. Recently she noticed that her two glasses of wine had turned into three or more, and she went home with some of her male colleagues on more occasions than she would like to admit.

Often on the mornings after a binge, Lauren would feel so embarrassed and guilty that she would stop at the store for a bottle of wine to drink away her feelings regarding the night before. She was late to work a few times because of a hangover and avoided certain work functions for fear that she would run into one of her one-night stands.

Lauren wanted to get married and began to wonder whether the guys she kept picking up were marriage material. A few of her friends expressed concern about how much she was drinking and the choices she was making. She wondered if perhaps it was time to talk to a counselor. But she would always get too busy and decide to wait until after the holidays or some other event.

Lauren was ambivalent about making changes. She was on the fence and not ready to do something anytime soon. A good friend or therapist should validate that Lauren is not sure whether she should make some lifestyles changes and let her know that any decisions she makes will be hers. The therapist should weigh the pros and cons of any changes with her and come up with a plan on how to deal with each. I would have her consider an answer to these questions: "If you were to make a change to your drinking, what would it look like?" and "What are you most concerned about if you decide to change how you drink?"

Giving Lauren unbiased education and information could also be helpful in assisting her to make a decision. If people are too harsh and confrontational, she may revert to denial, or she may feel bad and continue her drinking patterns secretly to deal with those negative feelings.

A person moves out of the stage of contemplation when making a conscious decision to change their alcohol behaviors.

Preparation

If you are in the preparation stage, you are ready to alter your drinking patterns. You have likely begun planning how to make the changes and are prepared to take action. You should think about the kind of changes you plan to make. Will you cut down or stop drinking completely?

In this stage, you have also sought the necessary resources. Some of them may include scheduling an appointment with a therapist, learning about moderation, going to an AA meeting, talking with your doctor about medications, going to rehab, or finding a support person. In the next several chapters, we will review specific actions you can take to help you be more successful in achieving your goals.

Dave was a thirty-eight-year-old computer programmer with two children. He worked long hours in the city and just wanted to unwind in the evenings with a few beers while he watched sports. Dave often fell asleep in front of the television and woke up hung over, not able to help with the kids or household chores. Last week his five-year-old son woke up early, found him passed out on the couch, and began building a fort with his father's empty beer cans.

Dave's wife often complained that he was not available to help with parenting, and they had not had sex in over two months because she was angry and resentful toward him. He had attempted to cut down on his drinking and even made it a few days without any beer. Later that week, Dave's wife sat him down and said that if he did not address his alcohol use, she was going to ask him for a separation. Dave believed she was serious this time, so the next morning he began looking up local therapists.

Dave recognized that he had a drinking problem. He did not want to admit it, but the threat of losing his family finally pushed him into action. He was motivated to make changes.

The goal here would be to help Dave identify obstacles to the change process and help him problem solve. He should identify his supporters. When he makes positive steps, like going several days without drinking or following through with attending meetings, he and his therapist should explore how he was able to do it. If the focus is on his successes, he can build upon that rather than only lament his failures. If he goes from daily drinking to drinking only three times that week, or from drinking a twelve-pack to drinking only two beers, those are successes. "How were you able to cut back?" "What did you gain?" and "What is your next step?" are important questions for him to answer.

Action

In the action stage, you make changes in your drinking patterns.

Tamika was a forty-five-year-old stay-at-home mother. She had been drinking since her teens. Tamika's childhood was not a happy one. It was filled with all the challenges that come from living with an alcoholic father and then being parented by an angry and depressed mother after their divorce.

As an adult, Tamika struggled with her own bouts of depression. She felt she had no identity and always had her guard up with her husband, fearing that he too would leave. She drank to help numb her feelings. She chose vodka because it gave her more bang for the buck, and she'd heard somewhere that the smell was less detectable.

Her two teenaged children began finding her hidden bottles around the house, and while her husband assured her that he loved her, he couldn't stand to see her in so much pain. During the past year, Tamika completed a five-day inpatient detox program, saw a therapist for her depression and unresolved issues from her childhood, and attended a weekly dual-diagnosis group with other adults dealing with addiction and its impact on their lives. For the first time in over twenty years, she began to like herself. Though she sometimes still sneaked a few drinks, she gave her family permission to let her therapist know so they could deal with it in treatment.

Over a lifetime, you may cycle through many of these stages. The coping skills that worked in the past may cease to help as new life challenges arise. Sometimes you may have the best intentions yet still struggle with maintaining the changes to your drinking patterns. The maintenance phase focuses on how to keep the changes going.

Maintenance

The maintenance stage occurs after you have changed your drinking patterns. The goal now is to keep the healthy behavior going to prevent a relapse to the old behavior. Many of my most successful clients schedule regular check-in appointments with me. These people have worked long and hard to get to where they are in their recovery process and do not want to go back to where they were. Some of them have chosen complete abstinence, and some are working on drinking in moderation.

Joe was a sixty-five-year-old who had just retired from a long career in the military and then the private sector. He was married and had three kids who had finished college and moved out to begin their own lives. He and his wife were finally living the life. They had retired to a warm climate, and Joe spent his days golfing and nights playing cards or shooting the breeze with friends.

Joe was a Scotch drinker. Throughout his life, he'd had periods where his drinking was too much, and he had actually attended two thirty-day inpatient programs, an intensive outpatient program, and AA meetings. In the last few years, he had been seeing a therapist who was helping him develop a moderation plan. The plan included drinking only one night of the week, not before 5 p.m., and never consuming more than three drinks at a time.

Joe had begun noticing that he was having a few beers on the golf course and that his neighbor was providing bourbon during their weekly poker games. Joe realized that both the amount and frequency of his drinking were creeping up again, and his wife was complaining that he was becoming moody and irritable. He made an appointment with his therapist and began reworking the moderation plan.

Joe had participated in many different forms of recovery treatments over the years. His drinking was not as bad as it had been at other times in his life, but he did not like the person he was becoming as his recent drinking increased. He and his wife had saved for a lifetime to be able to travel in their later years. If his alcohol intake continued to escalate, he worried that his health would begin to suffer, and he would not be able to enjoy his grandkids or take that European vacation.

Joe made a wise decision to check in with his therapist to rework his plan. Joe decided on a period of complete abstinence again. Once his system had been clean for a few months, he was able to have his weekly Scotch but eliminated beer on the golf course and the liquor during poker night. Both games improved greatly.

It is important to note that the stages described above can be looked at as a cycle that people often move through sequentially. However, Prochaska and DiClimente realized that although people often go through these stages in the described order, they also can skip a stage or move forward and backwards through them. I have found that we often cycle through the stages over a lifetime. We may resolve an issue, but then a crisis or a life change happens and we need to readjust to the stages.

Which stage do you think you are in right now? Why?

_____

_____

_____

What would it take to get you to the next stage? Who and what can help you?

_____

_____

_____

Have you gone through this cycle before? What worked for you then?

_____

_____

_____

Could you apply these skills to your current situation? What should you avoid doing again?

_____

_____

_____

INTERESTING INFO: Did you know many DUIs occur in the morning hours? Why is this? The average body processes alcohol at a rate of .016 BAC per hour. This is why many suggest that it is okay to have one drink per hour and still be able to drive. However, you must consider the number of hours you have been drinking. Many people try to be responsible after a night of heavy drinking and choose to stay where they are rather than drive. However, when they wake up in the morning, their body is still processing the alcohol. They may not feel drunk, but the alcohol is still in their system. If they drive and are pulled over, they may register a high Breathalyzer reading.

ANOTHER ROUND OF CHAPTER 5
Are You Ready to Make a Change?

- The Stages of Change model is very useful in determining which stage you or a loved one is in when thinking about changing drinking patterns.
- People often cycle through the stages over a lifetime.
- We need different types of assistance and accountability in each stage.
- Precontemplation is the stage when you do not think there is a problem with your alcohol use. To best help yourself in this stage, explore the impact of your drinking and acknowledge that you are not yet ready to make any changes.
- Contemplation is the stage when you acknowledge that there is a problem with your drinking and explore the steps needed to make a change.
- In the preparation stage, you are ready to make changes to your drinking patterns and may have researched steps to implement them.
- You are making the necessary lifestyle changes when you are in the action stage—woo-hoo!
- After you have made the appropriate lifestyle changes for your goal with drinking, your job is to figure out how to keep going and prevent a relapse. This is the maintenance stage.

Chapter 6

You Want Me to Do What?

A t this point, you should have a good understanding of how alcohol affects your brain and body. You have had an opportunity to self-assess—that is, figure out what type of drinker you are and the impact on your life. You may have decided that you would like to try to moderate your drinking. Not so fast! I believe in doing things the correct way, and you may not like what I am going to say right now. I recommend to all of my clients that before they try to moderate their drinking, they actually stop drinking for a period of time.

Hear me out: I recommend that before developing a moderate drinking plan, a person should attempt to remain totally abstinent from alcohol for four months. There is a method to my madness, and I will share my reasons with you in the pages following.

Why Four Months?

Some moderation programs recommend being clean for thirty days. I find this is often not long enough. Most of us can make a change for a short period of time but struggle to maintain it long-term. Of the many New Year's resolutions you have made, how many have actually become part of your day-to-day life? I am a regular gym user. In my gym, the classes fill up during the month of January and I often must wait to use the elliptical, or I have to search for the weights I want to use for a particular workout. However, by March I have my pick of all the equipment. That's because most people's good intentions fizzle out after a few weeks.

Have you ever tried to diet? I know I have. I give up my happy food—chocolate—and count my calories. I have successfully lost the pounds, only to eventually gain them back again. Why do so many of us struggle to make lasting change? We often give up behaviors that are not good for us, but we may not identify *why* we were making poor choices and *how* to maintain the positive changes. Some people claim that it takes twenty-one days to make a change. However, I believe it actually takes much longer when it comes to changing drinking habits.

INTERESTING INFO: The idea that it takes three weeks to form a habit is attributed to Dr. Maxwell Martz, a cosmetic surgeon. He reported in his book that it took patients an average of twenty-one days to get used to a new image after surgery. Over the years, this was misquoted so many times that people began to believe this was actually data from a study.

You may be familiar with the term *white knuckling*. Some say it originated with nervous flyers who gripped the armrests of their seats so tightly that their knuckles turned white. I believe many drinkers metaphorically do this. They hold on for a while and muscle through some alcohol-free time. Sometimes this is to prove to themselves or someone else that they don't really have a problem and can stop at any time. The concern is that during this time they may not be dealing with the internal reasons for their drinking, therefore not developing necessary coping skills.

In my practice, I actually want my clients to feel some discomfort during this period of abstinence. Yes, you heard me right. This gives us the opportunity to identify why they have been turning to alcohol. Once we know this, we can develop a reasonable plan of action.

Some people try to justify their drinking by saying they drink out of habit, not because of negative emotions like sadness or anger or to avoid something painful or uncomfortable. If this describes you, I would still recommend four months of not drinking. This will enable you to cycle through an entire season of events without alcohol in order to create a longer pattern. If you go four months without drinking, you will likely have to come up with a plan for handling holidays, birthdays, anniversaries, parties, sporting events, annual get-togethers, and other such events without relying on alcohol.

Ed was an intelligent, independent thirty-nine-year-old IT guy who was responsible for a large government department. The stress and long hours were killing him. He discovered that one or two beers helped him relax and fall asleep, but these soon turned into four or five beers and sometimes some bourbon as well. Ed was a runner and did not like the gut he was developing from the excessive drinking.

Ed came to me looking for help for his insomnia and stress. When I suggested that he might want to become alcohol free before we addressed those issues, he looked at me in horror, saying, "But how will I function? I can't sleep without it." I assured him that I wasn't asking him to start that night.

My job was to give him some tools to manage life better. I don't take away a client's primary coping skill of drinking (unless they need to be medically detoxed) before helping them to develop new ones. As Ed implemented new coping skills, he found he could fall asleep faster and actually had better quality of sleep without alcohol.

INTERESTING INFO: Did you know that alcohol is actually terrible for sleep problems? Some people think that drinking helps them fall asleep faster. This is not true. They are not falling asleep—they are passing out. Once they fall asleep, their quality of sleep is actually very poor. Alcohol reduces REM (rapid eye movement), the restorative dream sleep. The disruption to REM sleep may cause daytime drowsiness and poor concentration. Alcohol can also suppress breathing, thus increasing sleep apnea and snoring. Plus, sleep is interrupted because of having to get up to use the bathroom.

Clients often fight me about going through this period of abstinence. They argue that they are not alcoholics. I agree. Most of them are not. But they came to me because alcohol was causing some type of problem in their lives, whether it was a legal consequence, health related, a partner's complaint, or a friend's concern.

I encourage you to try abstinence for four months. After all, what do you have to lose? You know what it feels like to be a regular drinker, but what you don't know is what your current life will be like without drinking. If you hate it, you can always go back to the way life was before. However, you may be surprised at the new perspectives you gain about yourself and the people around you.

Getting SOBER

This next section will discuss some helpful skills to successfully abstaining from alcohol for four months.

Alcoholics Anonymous (AA) has a great acronym for sober:

Son
Of a
Bitch
Everything is
Real

If you are a drinker who is experiencing problems, this is exactly what I want for you. Deal with life on life's terms. You may need to gain some clarity so you can see the changes you need to make. Maybe your relationship isn't great because of your partner's anger concerning your drinking. Maybe with a period of abstinence, you will learn better communication skills that will lead to greater intimacy. It could be that you really should get a new job, but your drinking has been taking away this motivation. There might be an issue from your past that is still affecting you, and some work needs to be done to deal with it more effectively. During the abstinence period, you may also become bored and need to figure out different ways to have fun.

Boredom is one of the main causes of relapse. We all need something to look forward to each day, whether it is enjoying a good cup of coffee, working out, chatting with a coworker, snuggling with our mate, or watching our favorite show or sporting event. On a weekly basis, we need something that gets us excited. Maybe it's having dinner with friends, going to a movie, fishing on the weekend, or playing cards with the neighbors. We also should have bigger things to look forward to, like planning a getaway, crossing something off our bucket list, or taking a road trip.

One of my best friends has a great idea to help him experience life. He gets his local recreation guide and picks a number from one to whatever the number of pages in that quarter's issue. Then he opens the guide and picks an activity from that page. As a result, he has done some really cool activities, met some fun people, and has funny stories from the activities that were flops. The idea is to get out and do something. You may not like nine out of ten things you try, but the tenth one may become a new hobby or passion, and you may make some great friends along the way.

What things do you look forward to on a daily basis?

_____

What do you get excited about on a weekly basis?

_____

What do you do annually?

_____

Here's another way to get SOBER. I like the play on words because it helps me to remember things better. Below is a mindfulness-based relapse-prevention technique that breaks down the word *sober* and recommends steps for each of the letters:

S–STOP: Get out of autopilot mode. By this I mean stop doing things automatically without even being fully aware of what you are doing. For example, you get into your car to go run errands, and a few minutes later you somehow end up at the first store on your list. You did not consciously tell yourself to turn here, speed up, stop, go left, or park. Your brain just ran with the thought and got you there. This works well in neutral situations, but think of the times when you run on autopilot regarding unhealthy behavior. You get in the car and automatically light up a cigarette. Maybe you sit on the couch, turn on the television, and unconsciously finish a whole bag of chips. Many people do this with their drinking too.

Michele's goal was to remain abstinent from alcohol. She wasn't an alcoholic but did not like the consequences that her drinking caused on her health and her family. She had made it nine months without a drink. Then she attended a large family gathering in a restaurant. The table was set beautifully to include both water glasses and wineglasses. The server promptly filled both glasses for all adult guests.

Michele was happily chatting with her favorite cousins. She was so involved in the conversation that she did not notice that she had already drunk the entire glass of house white, which the waiter dutifully refilled. It was not until she got up to use the ladies' room that she realized she was a little tipsy. She was angry with herself, and her husband stared at her accusingly later that night.

Michele drank on autopilot. Though she had no intention to drink at this event, she had also made no active effort not to drink. If she had been more mindful, she may have been more successful in maintaining her sobriety. She could have had a conversation with her husband beforehand, asking for his support; asked the waiter to remove her wineglass; and ordered her favorite nonalcoholic beverage before she got swept up in the emotion of the event.

When do you typically go on autopilot?

_____

_____

_____

When is it damaging for you?

_____

_____

_____

What can you do the next time you are involved in a similar situation?

_____

_____

_____

O–OBSERVE: Observe your emotions, urges, physical sensations, and thoughts. In other words, know your triggers. Many drinkers spend a lot of time in an artificial emotional state—either thinking about drinking, being under the influence, or recovering from the impact of drinking. As you go into early abstinence, be aware that you may experience a heightened sensitivity to your environment, but this is not a permanent state. I share this because this is why many people give up abstinence in the early days. They think, "If this is what being alcohol free feels like, I don't want it."

Be aware of how you feel as you go into a drinking situation. You may notice certain reactions in your body before they actually become conscious thoughts. These may be signals that require your attention and action. The more aware you are of what is going on internally, the better you can deal with the external enjoinment. Understand that giving in to a momentary urge may not yield the best outcome for the long term.

The next time you are experiencing a craving or unhealthy desire, pay attention to the following:

How does your body feel physically?

_____

What do you feel emotionally?

_____

What do you want to do?

_____

What should you do?

_____

If you fail to prepare, you prepare to fail.

B–BREATHE: Pay attention to your breathing. Are you breathing in and out slowly and evenly? Are both your chest and your stomach rising and falling with each intake and exhale, or do you sometimes gulp for air? Do you sometimes hold your breath? Is your breathing rapid and shallow? Focus on your breathing; it can tell you a lot about how you are feeling.

Breathing is something we do unconsciously thousands of times a day. A change in normal breathing can signify that we are experiencing negative emotions. When we get upset, angry, scared, or nervous, we tend to go into fight-or-flight mode. In this reaction, the body either prepares to fight perceived danger or gears up to run away from it. The heart rate increases, stomach production shuts down, hormones are secreted, pupils dilate, and breathing rate speeds up.

A simple way to recognize when you might be in trouble emotionally is to check your breathing. If you are experiencing negative emotions, you will tend to breathe more quickly and more shallowly, more in the upper half of your chest. The simplest way to calm down this fight-or-flight reaction, which is an emotional and not a logical response, is to practice deep breathing. It is so simple, yet it unleashes a powerful calming response.

Ideally sit in a comfortable place without crossing your arms or legs. Place one hand on your chest and one hand on your stomach. The goal is to take in full, deep breaths, making sure that your stomach rises. If you are alone, you might want to close your eyes. Breathe in slowly for a count of five, hold for five seconds, and then release slowly on a count of five. Don't be surprised if the first time you try this, you feel a little dizzy and uncomfortable. This is just your body reoxygenating. The more you practice this technique before you get stressed, the lower your stress level will be and the less likely it will be for your emotions to escalate quickly.

If you were ever to catch me in traffic with my kids arguing in the backseat, you would see that I had one hand on the wheel and one on my stomach. I would be practicing deep breathing so I don't crash into the idiot in front of me or get involved in the sibling fight behind me.

E–EXPAND: Expand your awareness to your entire body and the area around you. Pay attention to your surroundings and how they make you feel. Identify any triggers that you are facing.

Practice doing a body scan. This simply means being aware of what you are feeling in your body. What thoughts are running through your mind? Do you feel any stress or tension in your head or face, your neck and shoulders? What is going on in your stomach? How does your back feel? Are you clenching your teeth, hands, or jaw?

If you are experiencing negative physical symptoms, take a moment to determine whether you could take action to address them. If you are feeling excitement, happiness, or relaxation, celebrate the feeling and figure out how you can repeat and increase it in a healthy way!

R–REACT: React mindfully. To react mindfully means being aware of both your internal and external experiences and making a conscious choice of what to do about them. Once you know what is going on in your mind and body, take the appropriate steps. Realize that sometimes you may not know what you are feeling or what to do. This is a great time to call a friend or partner or to post on a moderation forum and get some perspective. We often make things worse in our own heads, but people who know and love us can offer a different perspective, bring us back to reality, help us make decisions, and provide support. Whom do you trust to call in a crisis? Who in your life gives you great support? Once you figure out a good pattern, keep it going. Autopilot is not always a bad thing in regards to a healthy behavior.

Managing Risky Situations
Levels of Risk

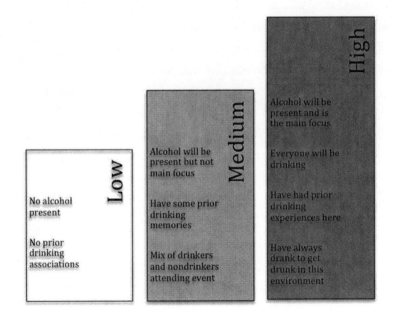

Alcoholics Anonymous (AA) and many treatment facilities recommend that problem drinkers give up all people, places, and things associated with substance use. I have a different approach. Because it is challenging to give up everything associated with alcohol use, I focus more on *levels of risk.* When we look at life in terms of black and white, we often give up because an all-or-nothing approach is unrealistic and too hard to maintain. I prefer to explore the shades of gray. I recommend that you evaluate people, places, and things and consider your level of risk associated with them.

LOW RISK: Alcohol is unlikely to be at this event, the people in attendance are not regular drinkers, and you have no past associations of drinking here. This is an environment that should be okay for you to be in. Just have a plan before you go, and be prepared for the unexpected.

MEDIUM RISK: Alcohol may be present at this event, but it is not the main focus. You may have consumed alcohol at this place in the past, but you also have nonalcohol-related memories of it and have friends there who will not be drinking. This is a situation that you could possibly attend, but you should have a plan and go with a support person.

HIGH RISK: You know that if you go to this bar, house, party, concert, casino, club, or sporting event, a lot of drinking will be taking place. You drank in these situations and with these people in the past. You have never participated in this event without consuming alcohol. As you are readjusting your drinking patterns, high-risk situations may be places to avoid until you are more confident and comfortable with your new plan.

Dan was one of my favorite clients in dealing with people, places, and things associated with drinking. He was a self-admitted alcoholic who drank to excess, had received several DUIs, blacked out frequently, and had lost things that were important to him, including his marriage and ability to drive a car. Dan participated in a very good recovery program that featured detox, individual therapy, dual-diagnosis group therapy, and regular AA attendance, including working AA's twelve steps and meeting with a sponsor.

One of Dan's closest childhood friends was getting married. The best man planned to have the bachelor party in Las Vegas. Dan's friends did not have an issue with alcohol; they planned to live it up as single men and do everything that often goes along with it. Dan's friends wanted him to go on the trip so badly that they offered to pay for a prostitute to stay with him to make sure he did not drink when they were out!

Dan realized that this trip was too high of a risk for him, and he decided not to go. He skipped the bachelor bacchanal but happily attended the weekend events for the wedding. He recently celebrated five years clean at one of his AA speaker's meetings.

What are low-risk situations for you? How can you prepare for them?

_____

_____

What are medium-risk situations for you? How can you make them less risky?

_____

_____

What are your high-risk situations? Should you avoid them? What could you do instead?

_____

_____

_____

_____

_____

Managing Cravings

Another goal in the early months of alcohol abstinence is developing self-regulation skills. This is learning how to tolerate negative emotions and delay rewards. Dr. Andrew Tatarsky, an expert on integrative harm-reduction psychotherapy, talks about "urge surfing." He calls this the ability to notice sensations and thoughts and breathe in to them. Just because we have a thought or feeling does not mean we have to take action.

Distraction can be a healthy way to manage cravings, both physical and mental. Our bodies may tell us we need alcohol, and our minds may play tricks on us, telling us that we need to drink in order to manage a thought or emotion. I always recommend having a plan in place before you actually need it. Sometimes just the act of knowing what to do in a crisis will help you feel more prepared for what to do when something actually does happen. Remember all those fire drills you participated in as a kid?

Check off some positive distractions that you could use when tempted to drink:

_____ Read a magazine

_____ Call a friend

_____ Leave a message for your therapist

_____ Play a computer game

_____ Watch a television show

_____ Listen to music

_____ Write down your thoughts

_____ Pray or meditate

_____ Take a walk

_____ Do your nails

_____ Take a bath

_____ Organize something

_____ Lift weights

_____ Do housework

_____ Reach out to your support person

_____ Play with your kids

_____ Surf the Internet

_____ Go to an AA, HAMS, MM, or SMART meeting

_____ Read recovery literature

_____ Review online moderation tools

_____ Make a post on a moderation forum

_____ Look up a yoga video on YouTube

_____ Say the Serenity Prayer

_____ Play it through (*If I have this drink, what will happen?*)

When you have a craving, ask yourself the following questions:

1. What am I feeling physically?

_____

Pay special attention to your head, neck, and stomach. These are the places where you will often experience the physical outlet of emotions. Explore what happened right before the urge. What does the urge want? If it could speak, what would it say to you right now? Is it trying to tell you something about yourself?

2. What am I thinking?

_____

Oftentimes you will experience a rush of many different thoughts. Pay attention to any self-defeating patterns. Take several deep breaths and imagine any negative thoughts being placed into the cargo hold of an airplane. Imagine the negative thoughts and patterns leaving so that you can focus on healthy, positive thoughts and patterns. The more senses you engage in a positive thought or image, the less able you are to think about the negative thought.

3. *What is a positive thought or image that I can focus on instead? What do I see, hear, feel, and smell?*

_____

_____

_____

Practice healthy distractions. Review the list above. When you experience a craving, do something different.

4. *What are my go-to healthy distractions?*

_____

Determine whether you need to take action. Sometimes you just need to acknowledge a craving and then focus on something else. Sometimes cravings are so intense that no amount of distraction seems to help. Reaching out to someone may be important to help you reality test, stay busy, and be accountable.

5. *If my positive distractions do not work, what action can I take?*

_____

Strategies for Change

If you have decided to make a change in your drinking habits, try the following steps before you are confronted with a situation:

First, identify a hypothetical situation. It might be a risky situation or something that increases a craving for alcohol.

Next, identify the skills needed to achieve your goal. Go back and review the things in this chapter that made sense to you.

Third, develop a plan and put it into action.

Finally, review the plan. How well did it work? Which parts would you do again? Which parts should be discarded in favor of something different? How would you like to handle the situation the next time it happens? Remember, it's not just about the alcohol; it's what the alcohol does for and to you.

INTERESTING INFO: Drinking coffee, going for a walk, or taking a cold shower will not help you sober up. On the average, it takes two to three hours for a single drink to leave the body. Nothing can speed up this biological process.

ANOTHER ROUND OF CHAPTER 6
You Want Me to Do What?

- In order to have the best chance of maintaining a successful moderate drinking plan, you should first commit to four months of total abstinence from alcohol.
- Being alcohol free for four months allows you to gain a clear perspective, identify problems, and develop coping skills.
- Having daily, weekly, and yearly things to look forward to prevents boredom.
- Get SOBER: **S**top, **O**bserve, **B**reathe, **E**xpand, **R**eact.
- Learn to recognize your low-, medium-, and high-risk situations. Develop a plan for when you encounter risky people, places, or things.
- Identify positive distractions for managing cravings.

Chapter 7

Taking and Interpreting the Quiz

*H*ere is what you have been waiting for—the quiz that will help you determine whether you can keep drinking. You have to be honest with yourself. I recommend going over the quiz with a neutral person. Even better would be to work with a trained therapist in the field of substance-use disorders, moderation, and mental health diagnosis and treatment.

HOW DO I KNOW IF I CAN KEEP DRINKING? QUIZ

For a person to consider continuing, reducing, or returning to drinking is a relatively new and controversial topic in the substance-use disorders field. It is a very individualized approach and needs to be discussed and monitored with someone who will offer you an unbiased approach and whose opinion you trust. Please answer the following questions honestly, and discuss them with your support person.

How long have I been drinking? _____

How many drinks a day do I have? _____

What are my medical issues? _____

What medications am I taking? _____

What have the consequences of my drinking been?_____

When I drink, what happens? _____

Why do I drink? _____

What is my goal in drinking? _____

What is the impact of my drinking on my family? _____

What supports do I have? _____

Do I have any co-occurring mental health concerns?

❑ Yes   ❑ No

Do I use any other drugs?

❑ Yes   ❑ No

Do I have any legal, probationary, or work issues?

❑ Yes   ❑ No

Have I had withdrawals from drinking?

❑ Yes   ❑ No

Am I willing to establish a period of abstinence?

❑ Yes   ❑ No

Am I willing to monitor my use of alcohol?

❑ Yes   ❑ No

Will I review my moderate drinking plan with someone?

❑ Yes   ❑ No

Interpreting the Quiz

Your answers to the "How Do I Know If I Can Keep Drinking? Quiz" will give you a better idea of whether you can consider a moderate drinking plan or whether you would be better off not drinking at all. Certain questions are positive predictors for success, while others offer lower chances of success in being able to drink moderately. The more positive predictors you have, the better the odds, and vice versa. If you have too many negative predictors, continuing to drink may be very risky for you. Please see the interpretation below.

I wish I could say that a certain score gives you a clear "yes" or "no" answer on the feasibility of your continued drinking. But you are a complicated individual with many facets. Plus, your current ability to drink moderately may be different from what it was ten years ago. A client of mine recently said that if he had read this book when he was in his thirties, he might not have become the self-admitted alcoholic he now is in his fifties.

How Long Have I Been Drinking? Beginning to drink before the age of fifteen is a strong negative predictor. One study of over forty thousand adults found that nearly half of the people who began drinking before the age of fifteen met the criteria for a severe alcohol-use disorder, while that percentage dropped to less than 10 percent if they waited until age twenty-one.

Researchers at the National Institute on Alcohol Abuse and Alcoholism (NIAAA) believe that alcohol more negatively affects younger teens' brains because they are not yet fully developed. Alcohol can lead them to make choices that focus more on immediate pleasure versus making choices that avoid the long-term impact that heavy drinking can bring. They found that individuals who begin drinking before the age of fifteen are four times more likely to develop dependence on alcohol than those who delay their first drink until the age of twenty. Delaying drinking until the age of twenty-one drops the rate of developing an addiction to 10 percent. Adults who took their first drink before the age of fifteen are seven times more likely to experience alcohol problems than those who delayed until the age of twenty-one.

In addition to the legal reasons, there are very real biological reasons to delay drinking until the age of twenty-one. Current research tells us that the brain is not fully developed until, on the average, age twenty-six. This is significant because of a process called *cell adaptation*. Cell adaptation refers to the changes made by a cell in response to adverse environmental changes. In other words, if a substance is introduced into a developing brain, the brain cells believe they need this substance to continue developing. If an underdeveloped brain is given alcohol, it will adjust and continue to need more and more of it to grow. This is what we call *tolerance*. Tolerance to alcohol is a negative predictor for the ability to moderately consume it.

The Centers for Disease Control and Prevention (CDC) report that most drinking under the age of twenty is in the form of binge drinking. The intent is to get drunk, not to enjoy the taste. Younger people are usually chasing the physical and social effects of alcohol and are not likely to consume only a moderate amount; thus the earlier alcohol is introduced, another reason for the higher the rate of addiction.

Another possible concern related to the early onset of drinking is the environment in which you were raised. Was alcohol a regular part of your parents' lives? Were drinks a part of all family celebrations? Was alcohol the main focus or just one of many beverages available? What were your family's views on drinking? Were they permissive? Did you have any family members who had alcohol-related problems?

Consider these responses for yourself as well as for any children you have or plan to raise or be around in the future. Children learn about the world from the adults who are around them the most.

Jorge was a shy young man. In accordance with his cultural upbringing, he lived at home until he was in his late twenties. He had saved up enough money and now wanted to see what it was like to live independently.

Jorge moved to a new area, but he was very shy and struggled to make new friends. He found out that going to happy hour at bars was a good way to meet people. He learned that after five or six drinks, his social anxiety disappeared and he could openly talk with anyone. This worked great until he got pulled over for a DUI.

While Jorge's drinking pattern classified him as a heavy drinker (having several binges a month, drinking more than five drinks at a time, and drinking multiple nights a month), he had not yet developed a tolerance to alcohol. This was likely due to the fact that he had delayed drinking until he was twenty-eight, when his brain was fully developed. Because his prefrontal cortex—the area of the brain that is last to develop and is responsible for thinking, memory, and judgment—was mature, he eventually realized that there were other, healthier ways to meet friends, and he found better ways to deal with his social anxiety.

One day Jorge took a risk and struck up a sober conversation with a neighbor. Together they participated in other nondrinking activities that allowed him to develop better social skills, which reduced his fear of talking to new people. He still goes to the occasional happy hour but no longer feels the need for the social lubrication. His new girlfriend and wallet are happy that he no longer is a regular at the local bar.

How Many Drinks a Day Do I Have? As noted in previous chapters, women who have more than one drink a day and men who have more than two are considered to be moderate drinkers. The larger the amount and the more frequently you drink, the harder it is to change this pattern. Drinking every day is a negative predictor. If you associate drinking with specific events, it may be more challenging to moderate your drinking. If nights and weekends signal drinking time to you, it will be very important to develop new associations.

Julia was in her fifties, worked full-time, and was now helping raise her single daughter's six-year-old son. On top of that, her father's health was declining, and he had to be moved into a nursing home. Julia was at the end of her rope. She found that martinis were a great way to deal with her stress. However, she noticed that she was going to the liquor store so often that the three clerks there greeted her by name. In addition, her daughter told her that her grandson had begun asking why Grandma acted funny at night.

Julia decided that she couldn't eliminate any of her responsibilities, so she needed to find other ways to deal with her stress. She joined her local gym and discovered yoga, as well as two other women who were dealing with similar life struggles. Together they picked at least one weekend day a month for a girls' day, took turns babysitting each other's grandkids, and went to lunch after visiting their parents so they could vent about their stressors.

Julia was not a lifelong drinker. Although she had begun drinking every day, it was due to situational stressors. Once she found other ways to manage the stress, she realized that she did not need the outlet of alcohol every day. Julia cut down her drinking to having martinis only when she went out for dinner. She is now enjoying more energy in the morning, no heartburn at night, and feeling more joy in her relationships.

What Are My Medical Issues? There are some obvious all-or-nothing predictors related to medical conditions. The most common include pregnancy, cirrhosis, elevated liver enzymes, diabetes, or cancer. There are many others that should be discussed with your doctor. Additionally, if you have high blood pressure, high cholesterol, or a weakened immune system, you probably are not a candidate for moderate drinking.

In chapter 4, you learned that alcohol can be chronic, progressive, and fatal. Although the health risks associated with heavy drinking can take years to develop, they also can make current conditions worse. I recommend an open conversation with your doctor so that you can make an educated decision on the amount of alcohol, if any, that is acceptable for your health.

<u>What Medications Am I Taking?</u> There are contraindications for drinking with many medicines and supplements. Some medications, when taken with alcohol, can intensify drowsiness and put you at risk for accidents, falls, and even death. These may include medications for heart disease, insomnia, pain relief, and colds, as well as medications for psychiatric conditions like depression, anxiety, bipolar disorder, ADHD, and schizophrenia. Alcohol interactions can also occur with over-the-counter medicines like antihistamines, pain relievers, cough medicines, and some herbal preparations. Alcohol is known to affect antibiotics, antidepressants, antiseizure medications, benzodiazepines (for anxiety), opiates (for pain), and beta-blockers (for heart or high blood pressure).

This medication list is by no means exhaustive. Please check with your doctor, psychiatrist, or pharmacist to determine the impact of alcohol on any medications you are taking. Many psychiatrists report that alcohol mixed with antidepressants reduces their effectiveness. You should make an educated decision on whether it is safe to drink and take certain drugs. Be aware that a combination of alcohol and some drugs, such as sleeping medications, benzodiazepines, and certain medications for depression, can have lethal consequences. I always recommend taking prescribed medications over taking a drink.

<u>What Have the Consequences of My Drinking Been?</u> This is where you really need to take an honest look at yourself. It can be hard, but it is very important to seek the observations and opinions of the people closest to you. If you have heard the same concern from one person more than once, it may be valid. If you have had the same complaint

from a number of people, it is likely true. It may be hard to hear, but feedback from others can let you know what it is like to be on the receiving end of your behavior, especially when you are not yourself or have been denying the effects of your drinking on you and those around you.

William and his partner James had been together for over ten years. He and James would often go out to the clubs and imbibe in the nightly specials. After several years of working hard, they were able to purchase a house that they turned into their home. William still preferred to go out, but James liked to stay in.

The couple often hosted monthly dinner parties. William was the social butterfly, always with a drink in his hand and a story to tell. However, William and James had begun fighting more, especially about William's going out. James was concerned, not only about what William was doing in the clubs, but also that he would often stay out until the early morning hours. His trust in his partner was decreasing, and their sex life took a turn for the worse. Not as many friends were attending their parties. William would often get loud and rude, while James was left making apologies and cleaning up after everyone.

Problem drinking is not always as obvious as a DUI, a loved one ending a relationship, or health issues. Drinking can affect the quality of our relationships. Intimacy may decrease, fights may occur, and ongoing tension can damage a couple's happiness.

<u>When I Drink, What Happens?</u> This again is a hard question to answer honestly. Often denial kicks in and you tend to minimize what happens when you are inebriated. If you always seem to end up in a physical fight with your brother, engaged in a philosophical debate that leads to screaming, passed out snoring on the couch, or if someone else

always seems to end up crying, it may be a good idea to look at alcohol's contribution to the problem. Only you and the people closest to you can determine if your drinking is a problem. As I said previously, if it causes a problem, it is a problem.

If you have had a blackout, this is a very negative predictor for continued use of alcohol. There are two kinds of alcohol-related blackouts. The first is associated with alcohol abuse. This type may occur once or twice before the individual learns his limits and decides not to make the same mistake again. This is often seen in the teenaged or college drinker who consumes a large quantity of alcohol in a short period of time. Blackouts occur when they play drinking games that involve taking shots, participate in butt chugging or eyeballing, play beer pong, or consume a specific amount of alcohol as the loser of a drinking game.

The other type of blackout, which is more concerning, occurs on a more regular basis in the heavy drinker. The large amount of alcohol consumed prevents the brain from forming long-term memories, and the drinker loses a chunk of time. This is not forgetting a few things you said last night, but losing a few hours, not remembering things you did or how you got home. This is extremely dangerous because you may take risks that you normally would not, such as taking other drugs, going home with a stranger, or driving a car.

A blackout indicates brain damage. Alcohol is preventing the brain from encoding experiences and turning them into long-term memories. If you have had repeated blackouts, it is a negative predictor for your ability to moderate your drinking; your body may have developed a tolerance to drinking. For most people, a safety valve will turn on and they will do one of several things when they drink excessively. They will consciously decide to stop consuming drinks, pass out (fall asleep), or throw up. Most people do not and are not able to drink to the point of having a blackout.

<u>Why Do I Drink?</u> It is very important to understand why you drink, and the possible reasons are many. If it is to escape from feelings or an unpleasant situation, this is a negative predictor. It will be important for you to develop coping skills to deal with any underlying psychiatric issues like depression, anxiety, obsessive-compulsive disorder, or insomnia. If you are drinking to avoid problems in a relationship, job, or living situation, it is time to evaluate the environment. See if you can make acceptable changes to the situation, or examine whether it is time to leave the job or relationship. Therapy can be very helpful in working through these issues.

Lee was a fifty-one-year-old entrepreneur. He was intelligent, successful, and had all the trappings of success that a man could want: beautiful wife, three healthy kids, and enough money to take several vacations a year. But he could not seem to get a handle on his depression. He would get drunk to deal with feelings of sadness and worthlessness.

Lee scared himself the night he drove home after a business meeting and could not remember how he got there the next morning. He spent the next several months in individual therapy, addressing issues that had haunted him from childhood. Because he was still struggling with symptoms, he also sought the help of a psychiatrist to find the right antidepressant that significantly reduced his symptoms without causing serious side effects.

Lee chose to go through a period of abstinence from alcohol. During this time he developed better coping and communication skills, but he really missed wine. He was one of the rare people who could tell the difference between a $10 bottle and a $100 bottle. He developed a moderate drinking plan that allowed him to drink his favorite wines only in social situations and never more than two glasses at a time.

If Lee noticed the frequency of his drinking increasing, or if his depression symptoms began affecting his day-to-day life, he first talked it over with his wife. Lee trusted her opinion, and she was able to give support without criticism. If he did not feel better in two weeks, he would schedule an appointment with me to come up with strategies to help him feel better again.

What Is My Goal in Drinking? Do you drink to get drunk? Are you reluctant to make changes in your friendships and environment? Do you drink to be part of the social atmosphere? Again, if you drink to change your mood, it is a negative predictor. If you drink as part of a holiday or social gathering and are not trying to change your mood or emotions, it is a more positive predictor. Even better is if you simply appreciate a fine wine that brings out the flavor in your food, enjoy a cold beer on a summer day, savor the flavor of an aged liquor, or relish making a toast with champagne. Not trying to derive a certain effect from alcohol is a positive predictor.

What Is the Impact on my Family? If your drinking is causing problems in your primary relationships, you may have to decide which is more important to you. Parents also need to be honest concerning the messages about alcohol that you are sending to your children. Do you want your children to have the same relationship with alcohol that you do? Realize that kids are sponges. Parents set the example for what is normal because they are the primary adults in their children's lives; what their children see them do is imprinted on their brains as normal. All other experiences will be compared to these early first observations and impressions.

If your children are adolescents, they may begin to experiment with alcohol. You do not want to get stuck in the trap of "Do as I say, not as I do." You will lose all credibility. The teenagers I see in my adolescent dual-diagnosis program report little respect for parents who yell at them for going to a party and drinking, while they are holding their own glass of alcohol and slurring their speech from one too many.

Zeke was a seventy-two-year-old father of two and grandfather of five who was looking forward to celebrating his golden anniversary with his wife. He admitted that when he was in his thirties, he was an alcoholic. As a result, he became a regular AA participant and even sponsored new members. After several years, he stopped attending meetings, believing he had heard and said it all.

After almost twenty years of sobriety, Zeke wondered if he finally had this thing licked and could be "normal" again. To Zeke, "normal" meant that he could drink like most people, without consequences and able to stop with one or two glasses. However, when Zeke drank, it was in secret. One of his favorite places to drink was in the car. It gave him a double adrenaline rush. After a few months and too many close calls, he realized how dangerous this was for him and confessed to his wife. He decided to stop drinking liquor but still had the occasional glass of wine.

Zeke was never drunk again, but every time his wife saw him with alcohol or smelled it on his breath, she reverted right back to the misery of the earlier years of his heavy drinking. Zeke decided that his wife's happiness and well-being were more important to him than drinking. They just celebrated their fiftieth anniversary, and they toasted each other with sparkling cider.

<u>What Supports Do I Have?</u> Research shows that the number one predictor of success for a person's ability to moderate his drinking is having a good support system. There are many reasons for this. One is that people with a good support system tend to be happier and have lower rates of mental health issues. A support system also helps people stay accountable. When you look in the eyes of someone you love, they can often feel your guilt, and you want to be a better person for them.

This is why the best weight-loss programs include some form of accountability, which in turn leads to more goals achieved. If you have to share a food journal with a nutritionist, you are more likely to think about what you put into your body. And the scale does not lie—it knows when you have had too many chips or cookies. The same can be true with keeping a drinking diary. Writing how often, how many, and the impact of your drinks can be very telling.

<u>Do I Have Any Co-Occurring Mental Health Concerns?</u> The National Alliance of Mental Illness (NAMI) reports that as many as 40 percent of all people who misuse alcohol have a co-occurring mental health diagnosis. If you struggle with depression, bipolar disorder, anxiety, schizophrenia, post-traumatic stress disorder, or obsessive-compulsive disorder and drink, this is a negative predictor. However, once these issues are stabilized, you may be better able to explore whether moderate drinking is for you.

NAMI notes that drinking can be a way of self-medication—that is, people seek the effects of alcohol as a way to make their symptoms less painful. However, alcohol can actually worsen underlying mental illness while the person is under the influence or during withdrawal from alcohol. Drinking can make the symptoms of depression worse and increase panic attacks, not only from the actual chemical use, but also from the consequences of drinking. Additionally, alcohol use can trigger the onset of psychosis.

As noted above, it is critical to address any mental health issues before trying to drink moderately. This can be done in a variety of ways. It may be by developing better coping skills, getting out of a bad relationship or situation, seeking appropriate medication, resolving issues with a therapist, developing meaning in some form of spirituality, or learning new ways to relax and have fun. There is no quick fix and no one answer. You will likely need to address many areas of your life, but any investment in yourself should result in a healthier, happier version of you.

<u>Do I Use Any Other Drugs?</u> The use of any other non-prescribed mind-altering substances is a negative predictor. As noted previously, if you use a substance in order to change your mood, you are likely to stay in that pattern. A great saying is this:

If you do what you always did, you get what you always got.

John was a single thirty-three-year-old alcohol and marijuana user. He had decided that his drinking was causing him a lot of problems. He had developed quite a beer belly, suffered from high cholesterol and high blood pressure, and had to take medications for them. He wanted to be in a relationship but had no motivation to go out and find someone.

When John realized that most of his paychecks were going to beer and weed, he decided to get some help. He began therapy. His group members offered him great support and accountability, but he was reluctant to address his marijuana use. He said it was a natural substance and smoking it did not have any negative effects on him.

Six months later John was abstinent from alcohol but still smoked pot several times a week. He held the same hourly-paying job, played video games for fun, and had no girlfriend. He couldn't figure out why nothing had changed. Had he stopped smoking marijuana, he might have had a better chance to evaluate his life and been more proactive in his life goals. Because he was still using a mind-altering substance, he was unable to gain enough clarity to fully evaluate his life.

<u>Do I Have Any Legal, Probationary, or Work Issues?</u> These are obvious negative predictors. If your freedom, driver's license, or job is on the line, you cannot keep drinking. Once the probationary period has passed, you can explore a moderate drinking plan. The previous chapter offered tips on how to attain abstinence for now.

Have I Had Withdrawals from Drinking? If you have had delirium tremens, "the shakes," you cannot safely drink again. If you have had hallucinations or delusions (seeing or hearing things that are not there), these are serious symptoms that are very negative predictors for being able to moderate your dinking.

Remember that tolerance to and suffering withdrawal from alcohol indicate a severe drinking issue. There is therefore much less of a chance that you can keep drinking safely and moderately. It is possible but comes with very high risk. You have to evaluate why continuing to drink is so important to you. I would recommend speaking with a therapist trained in addiction treatment and moderation to help you make this very important decision.

Am I Willing to Establish a Period of Abstinence? As noted in chapter 6, before you try to moderate your drinking, you should first remain totally alcohol free for a period of four months. One of the main reasons is so that you can see how you handle a wide variety of situations without alcohol. During this time, you may experience discomfort. The goal is to learn other coping skills besides using alcohol. Being chemically free helps bring emotions to the surface, thus giving you an opportunity to manage life in a different way.

While you are alcohol free, you may find yourself focusing only on negative emotions such as anxiety, stress, depression, boredom, and anger. Don't forget to notice the emergence of positive feelings that perhaps had been numbed by alcohol: joy, awe, love, compassion, and empathy. The range of emotions that you experience when you are chemically free may pleasantly surprise you.

Additionally, sometimes we just fall into unhealthy patterns. This period of abstinence should give you enough time to break these patterns and determine to what degree—if any—you want alcohol to be part of the next stage of your life. In fact, 30 percent of those who try a period of abstinence decide to continue with permanent abstinence. Once you know you can do it, it is not as big of a deal to choose it voluntarily. Drinking or not drinking becomes less of a focus when you shift your attention, time, and activities to other opportunities. I recommend that you say "I choose not to drink" rather than "I can't drink." The former implies empowerment rather than deprivation.

As you began reading this book, you may have recognized that your current alcohol use has become a problem. You may have hoped for an easy way to cut down on your drinking without having to totally quit drinking. Nonetheless, I do recommend being alcohol free for a period of time. Going through a period of abstinence offers the following benefits:

- The safest known level of alcohol is no alcohol. If you do not drink, you do not face any further health, legal, social, or family problems.

- Being clean offers you perspective. It is an opportunity to see how you think, feel, and act in a variety of situations without the effects of alcohol.

- Abstinence allows you to more naturally feel your emotions. This gives you an opportunity to learn other ways to deal with them more effectively and without distraction.

- Not drinking gives you a chance to break habits, experience a change, and build your confidence to live without alcohol.

- Being alcohol free can help you identify triggers related to your use.

- Being clean helps you see the problems you were trying to avoid through your use of alcohol.

- Not drinking may allow the medications you are taking to work more effectively, thus reducing the need to drink in order to deal with symptoms.

Sal, a self-employed mechanic in his forties, stared at me in shock. I had just recommended that he try four months of abstinence. I said that the purpose was to feel the discomfort that he had been drinking away and see what new feelings emerged. He didn't jump up and leave the room, so I let him know that during the four months of abstinence, we would observe together what he was experiencing, and that I would help him develop coping skills as well as identify how and when positive ones surfaced so that he could repeat those.

I let him know that I would be his biggest cheerleader when he experienced success and would teach him how to build upon the wins. I also told him that I would kick him in the ass (not literally!) if he continued to make poor decisions. In this way, I offered him not only support and encouragement, but also the necessary accountability for when he felt hopeless or his willpower wavered.

<u>Am I Willing to Monitor My Alcohol Use and Be Accountable to Someone?</u> Who in your life has what you want? Identify those qualities and figure out how to emulate them. Find a mentor who can help you be honest with yourself, track your goals, and help you find solutions. This may be a friend, Moderation Management posting, an AA sponsor, professional therapist, person in recovery, spiritual leader, or loved one.

Be honest with yourself, and give the person a copy of your moderation plan, which will be developed in the next chapter. Give them permission to challenge you and confront you if you do not stick to your plan. Your job is to be open to their feedback. The support person should be strong enough to handle any resistance you might give when you are having a tough time. Your support person needs to be able to give you guidance. That person should also be willing and able to share in your success—and not with a celebratory drink!

INTERESTING INFO: The World Health Organization has found that alcohol use among women has been steadily increasing along with economic development and changing gender roles. Women are becoming more educated and thus earning more money—and spending it on alcohol. This is one instance where equality has not yielded the best outcome.

ANOTHER ROUND OF CHAPTER 7
Taking and Interpreting the
"How Do I Know If I Can Keep Drinking? Quiz"

It's time to go back and review your answers. Just as there are many personalities and problems, there are an infinite number of solutions. I want to offer you some general guidelines that are appropriate for most people:

1. The later you delayed drinking, the better predictor for you to successfully moderate your drinking.

2. If you drink every day and have multiple drinks at a time, this may be a negative predictor for your ability to continue drinking.

3. If you have any medical issues or take medications, it is important to check with your health-care providers to identify any contraindications between your health and continued drinking. If you have any health complications directly related to your drinking, you should not attempt to moderate your drinking but must focus instead on complete abstinence.

4. You should take a personal inventory of the consequences of your drinking on both you and the people around you. You must repair any damage caused by your alcohol use. You must also determine to what degree even a reduced amount of drinking will affect your health, family, job, and activities of daily living.

5. It is important to determine why you were drinking at the amount and frequency you were. Did you find solutions for

any of those problems? Were you drinking to achieve a desired effect? If so, this is a negative predictor. If you were drinking for taste, to enhance food, or as part of a celebration or social gathering, it is a more positive predictor for continuing alcohol consumption.

6. If you have any mental health concerns, you should address them with someone who understands when and how moderate drinking is possible and decide with them if it is safe for you to drink.

7. It is a negative predicator if you are abusing other drugs and want to continue drinking. Combining two or more mood-altering substances can be very dangerous for your health and safety and is often illegal.

8. You first need to satisfy any legal, probationary, or work issues related to your alcohol use prior to establishing a moderate drinking plan.

9. Withdrawal symptoms from alcohol almost always indicate a significant drinking problem and mean it is unlikely that you will be successful in attempting moderate drinking. Because your tolerance to alcohol has changed your physiology, it may not be possible to go back to a normal rate after a period of abstinence. Remember that once you transform from a cucumber to a pickle, you can't go back to being a cucumber again, no matter how badly you or other people want it.

10. If you have tried a period of abstinence and have successfully managed the emotions, people, places, and things connected with your drinking, you are a better candidate for moderate drinking.

11. If you are willing to monitor your use of alcohol and be accountable to a support person, you are much more likely to be successful in moderate drinking.

Chapter 8

Moderate Drinking Plan

Congratulations! If you have made it this far, it means the following:

- You have educated yourself about the biological, psychological, and social consequences of your drinking on both you and the people in your life.
- You have not developed a physical dependence on alcohol.
- You can commit to not engaging in unsafe behavior after drinking any amount of alcohol, such as driving a vehicle, operating machinery, caring for another person, and other such things.
- You do not misuse other mood-altering substances.
- You do not act in self-destructive ways after drinking even a small amount of alcohol.

- You have experienced a period of abstinence.
- You have identified your triggers and made a plan to deal with risky situations.
- You have experienced a range of emotions and learned how to cope with negative ones and enhance positive feelings in healthy ways.
- You have determined that it is safe for you to continue drinking.
- You have chosen a support person to review your moderate drinking plan and help keep you accountable to it.

If you have not figured these out or just skipped ahead to this section, you are shortchanging yourself. Go back and reread the previous chapters. You will find a lot of important information to help you figure out the role drinking has played in your life as well as give you tools to assist in changing your life. You and your loved ones deserve the healthiest and happiest version of yourself.

How would you ideally like to drink? Have you identified whether that is realistic? Your next steps will help you determine how to monitor risks and consequences and with whom you will review them.

Remember that moderate drinking is less than fourteen drinks a week for men and less than eight drinks a week for women. This does not mean that you get to drink all the drinks on one night! This would classify you as a binge drinker, which has its own consequences, including poor decision making, accidents, fights, and legal charges.

If reduced drinking is your goal, honest self-reporting is crucial. If you have developed and are invested in your moderate drinking plan, you will be more motivated and more likely to be truthful about whether the plan is working. If you are trying moderate drinking, the goal should not be to get drunk. Celebrating or enjoying the taste of alcohol is okay, but you have to know when you cross the line. For most people, this means having no more than two or three drinks over several hours, and not doing shots.

Below is a sample moderate drinking plan. Fill it out and share it with your support person. Some items may not be appropriate for you, and you may want to add other topics. Consider your answers and whether you should have a plan of action for each topic.

MODERATE DRINKING PLAN

I am choosing to keep drinking because:

_____

_____

I will not drink in these situations:

_____

_____

_____

I will not drink until:

_____

I will not drink after:

_____

I will not drive after consuming:

_____

I will alternate an alcoholic beverage with:

_____

I will have no more than _____ drinks per: _____

I will not drink at all under these conditions:

I will review my plan with:

If I/we notice:

I/we will:

   By this point, you have had the chance to take an honest look at your consumption patterns and the impact of your drinking and determined that you can safely consider a moderate drinking plan. Let's look at how to make it a reality. The websites moderation.org and hamsnetwork. org offer some great tools in developing and monitoring a plan. Realize that your moderate drinking plan is not written in stone. However, this does not give you permission to cheat. Rather, your plan should be a fluid document that adapts as your life changes. The initial plan may include trial and error based on what works for your lifestyle and possible relapses.

   A relapse in problem behavior is not always a bad thing. It is an opportunity to address areas that you may not have considered or been realistic about when you first developed the plan. A relapse is a signal that something is not working and you need another strategy. Sometimes relapses can help everyone to take the situation more seriously. It is easy to get lulled into comfort when you actually need to be more on guard and prepared for how to handle drinking situations.

Preparing to Drink Again

If you have made it through a period of time without drinking—congratulations! A lot of hard work, planning, thinking, and dealing with emotions went into this accomplishment. You probably spent a large amount of time learning how to stop drinking. But what happens after you complete your period of abstinence and prepare your moderate drinking plan? I have found, unfortunately, that very few professionals or programs help you prepare for what life may be like when you start drinking again.

Amy was in her mid-twenties. After a period of significant emotional and relationship turmoil resulting from her drinking, she finally made the healthy decision to complete a thirty-day rehab program. After rehab, she resumed her weekly individual therapy and worked very hard to find new ways to have fun, utilize the coping skills she had learned but had never been able to put into practice, and set boundaries in relationships.

After she had been substance free for over six months, we used therapy sessions to prepare her for moderate drinking. She chose a specific drink that she actually enjoyed the taste of, met with a healthy friend who supported her drinking goals, and chose an environment where she had never had a bad drinking or emotional episode.

Amy was not prepared for the emotions stirred up by losing her clean date (day after last substance use). She no longer felt the special feeling that sobriety had brought to her life. She had been keeping track of the days that marked the end of her unhealthy life and the start of a new one.

Amy was also not prepared for the feelings of guilt that surfaced. During the time when she was not drinking, she had felt as if she were making up for all the poor decisions and actions that had hurt her friends and family. Once she had the first drink, however, she felt as though she had lost their forgiveness.

Through unexpected tears, Amy realized she had more work to do. She decided to remain alcohol free for a few more months while she worked on her feelings about dealing with her past, repairing her current relationships, and identifying who she would like to be in the future.

Treatment programs tend to focus on getting clean of substances, not necessarily on how to stay clean. Getting clean looks at what not to do; staying clean needs to address the emotional aspects of the process. In the scenario above, Amy was going through a process that I call *integration*. Integration is accepting who you were and what you did when you were drinking in an unhealthy way. It means not only seeking forgiveness from those you hurt, but also forgiving yourself.

People in early recovery tend to spend a lot of time reliving the past, which was often destructive, unhealthy, and emotionally painful. While it is important to acknowledge the mistakes of the past, we cannot live there if we are going to stay healthy in the long run. The same is true for the present. It is important to stay connected and mindful of what is happening in the moment, but we also need to prepare for a healthier, happier future. It is only once we integrate our past self into who we are in the present that we really begin to move forward emotionally. When I see people feeling comfortable with who they are right now and getting excited about something in the future, I know they have completed the integration process.

QUICK CHECK FOR SUCCESS OF
MODERATE DRINKING PLAN

A simple gut check when evaluating the success of your moderate drinking plan is to ask yourself the following questions:

1. *What is the amount that I have been consuming?*

_____

2. *What is the intent of my moderate drinking?*

_____

3. *What is the impact of my current alcohol use?*

_____

4. *How frequently have I been drinking?*

_____

Let's break down the importance of focusing on the *amount, intent, impact,* and *frequency* of your current drinking patterns. Though you have reached the point where you have developed a moderate drinking plan, it has likely taken you a while to get here. You and your loved ones have likely struggled with a lot of emotional pain and consequences. You may have attempted several traditional treatments that made you feel like a failure because you were not able to remain completely abstinent from alcohol.

To be implementing this moderate drinking plan, I assume that you have engaged in a great deal of interpersonal exploration and change. You have worked hard, and I want you to be successful. And, I admit, I would love for you to prove wrong the people who believe that total abstinence is the only way to recovery.

Quick Check

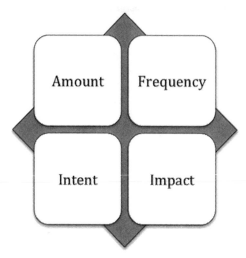

Amount

Keep in mind all the guidelines we discussed for amount and frequency of alcohol consumption and when it is considered a problem. You need to pay attention to how many drinks a day and/or week you are consuming. I know this is repetitive, but for men that means no more than fourteen drinks a week, and for women no more than eight a week and not all at the same time. The people who experience the greatest success usually drink no more than once a week, never drink alone, and consume no more than three drinks at a time. You have to figure out what is realistic for you.

How do I know if it is too much? you may be thinking. Consider the following questions to help you come up with an answer:

How many nights a week do you drink?

Do you drink more than two drinks a night if you are a woman, or more than three if you are a man?

Do you feel an effect from the alcohol? Pay attention to what you notice on the days of consumption and the days following.

Also pay attention to how much you are focusing on your "drinking days." If it is what gets you through the day, you still have some work to do. Explore what is so bad about your day-to-day life that you crave this outlet. See if you can develop other things you look forward to doing.

You may be tempted to make exceptions to your moderate drinking plan. Holidays, graduations, weddings, birthdays, free tickets to a game, and sports playoffs will come up. However, there is no reason you cannot enjoy these events without alcohol. Find something other than alcohol to focus your attention on: the people, the game, the food, or the celebratory aspect of the event.

This brings us to the second area of focus: intent.

Intent

Be cognizant of *why* you are drinking. As noted previously, if you are looking to change your mood or to cope with emotions, you lack sufficient coping skills. Find someone who has his or her life together. Observe what they do and how they do it. See if you can emulate some of their skills. Identify which ones work for you.

If you are feeling an effect from the alcohol you consume, you should reevaluate the amount you are taking in. Identify why you place such a high priority on drinking. Pay attention to how you feel when you drink. If this is the only time you are happy or feel normal—you guessed it—you have more work to do. It may mean that it is time to talk with a therapist to explore what is missing from your life and how to find it in a healthy way.

Notice how you feel on nondrinking nights. If you feel bored, miserable, and left out, you will need to reevaluate your plan. You should find other ways to relax, socialize, and have fun. This may take time, especially if your past alcohol consumption has damaged some of the neurotransmitters in your brain that allow you to feel pleasure and happiness. It takes time to repair the effects that alcohol has had on your body chemistry. The good news is that with mindful effort and activity, you can learn to feel good again.

Ask your family and friends for their observations about you now that you have changed your drinking patterns. They may be able to share with you behaviors and observations that you cannot yet recognize.

Also, if you are struggling on your nondrinking nights, you may not have allowed yourself enough time to adjust to your new lifestyle. Any change takes time to feel normal. It may take several months for your reduced drinking to feel normal, but most people report feeling significantly better after six months, and certainly by a year.

Impact

Not to remind you about all the bad times related to your problematic drinking patterns, but have you avoided the previous consequences from your drinking as you have implemented your moderate drinking plan? If they are recurring, you will need to reevaluate. Look at what happens now when you drink. If you are not getting the "stink eye" from your family members, no one is complaining, and you are happy, you may have developed a very good plan. Take a risk and ask your loved ones for their observations on your current drinking. You may be pleasantly surprised to hear what they have to say about you now.

Be realistic with whose opinions you consider. Asking your old drinking buddies how you are doing with your new drinking pattern will yield very different responses from those of the people you live with and may have hurt.

Frequency

Continuing to drink on a daily basis tends to be very risky. About half of the problem drinkers who decide to moderate their use go back to heavy drinking. It may be that they did not honestly answer the questions in the "How Do I Know If I Can Keep Drinking? Quiz," did not implement the right tools, were genetically predisposed to have a drinking problem, or body chemistry had changed as a result of chronic drinking. You may have to adjust your goals in the future if a severe consequence occurs.

As noted in chapter 1, people may vacillate on the spectrum of alcohol use over the course of their lives. Several of my clients have acknowledged that had they changed their drinking patterns years earlier, they may have been able to moderately drink now, but by the time they realized they needed to make a change, things had progressed too far for them to ever safely drink again.

Moderation Tools

Here are some tools to help you moderate your drinking:

- Drink only in social situations.
- Pick a favorite nonalcoholic drink.
- Never drink alone.
- Know before you go somewhere how much you plan to consume.
- Rotate between drinking a nonalcoholic beverage and one with alcohol.
- Avoid high-risk situations.
- Bring an accountability partner with you when you go out.
- Keep a drink diary or chart, paying attention to when you drink, how much you drink, and how you feel before and after you drink.
- When you drink, sip slowly and mindfully.
- Offer to be the designated driver when out with others.
- Put your watch or a bracelet on the wrist of the hand that typically holds your drink as a visual reminder of the limits you chose.
- Do not drink when you are upset.

- Plan an early event for the next day after drinking.
- Have a statement prepared that explains to others why you are not drinking, and practice it ahead of time.
- Wear the number of bracelets or rubber bands that corresponds to the number of drinks you plan on having, and remove them as you consume the drinks.
- Make sure to eat before you drink.
- Set an alarm on your phone so that you leave an event before it gets out of control.
- Know your triggers.
- Write down your reasons for making changes to your drinking patterns. Review them before you go out.
- Plan to check in with a friend while you are out and when you return.
- Determine a time to review the successes and failures of your plan.
- If these suggestions seem punitive to you, you may not be ready to try moderate drinking.

Craig had worked in the restaurant industry for most of his life, so drinking was a big part of special occasions for him. One day in a therapy session, he was lamenting that he would be celebrating his birthday during his period of abstinence. He had always looked forward to hanging out with the regulars and having them buy him a drink rather than him making one for them. Given that he had bartended for years, I suggested he create a "mocktail," a nonalcoholic mixed drink. I could see the wheels turning in his mind as we ended the session.

The next week, he came in proudly for two reasons. One was that he had celebrated his birthday alcohol free, finally sticking to his commitment after many failed attempts. And two, he had created a new mocktail that was going to be added to the restaurant's menu and named after him!

Tangible Reminders

Utilize tangible reminders—things you see, feel, touch, and hold—that remind you of why you are making changes to your drinking patterns. Some positive reminders may include the following:

- A picture of the house you want to buy with your loved one if you resolve the problems related to your alcohol use
- The car you want to drive once your license is reinstated
- A photo of your kids on your last vacation when you were sober and got up early to play with them on the beach
- A mug from the school you want to attend or the place you hope to work

Motivational reminders could include these:

- Putting a sticky note of the Serenity Prayer on the dashboard of your car
- Keeping a clean-date countdown on your phone
- Having an AA chip in your pocket
- Reviewing an inspirational quote each morning

Use negative reminders. While most of us are more motivated by positive reminders, remaining aware of the consequences of drinking is very important as time passes and denial kicks in.

- Keep the business card of your therapist or probation officer where you will see it before you open your wallet to pay for alcohol at the liquor store.
- Place the bracelet from your last hospital stay after your accident in the area where you keep your wine or highball glasses.

- Write down all the reasons you changed your drinking patterns, and review them the next time you experience a craving.

Choose what is meaningful to you, and keep these reminders in places that will stand out to you.

Another activity you could do is to calculate the dollar amount you typically spent on alcohol in a given day: perhaps $20 a day on wine or liquor or a $60 bar tab. Identify something that you would like to treat yourself with: a massage, round of golf, new purse, or tickets to a game. Go to the bank and get $10 bills in the amount of what you would like to have in order to treat yourself. Find a clear container and place it near your alcohol or the glasses you drink from. Place the jar in one of those two places. For each day that you do not drink, put a ten in the container. For every day that you drink when you were not supposed to, take $20 out of the container. At the end of a designated period of time, use the cash saved by making better choices to enjoy your special treat. This is a great tangible representation of how much you were spending on alcohol and how making small choices every day can add up to something positive.

Which one of these reminders will you try? What are other ones you could also use?

_____

_____

_____

Would You Like a Drink?

Where did your mind go when reading the question above? Did you think about beer, wine, or a mixed drink, or did you think *I'll have water, soda, or coffee*? Many times regular drinkers who become abstinent or change their drinking patterns are very worried about how other people will react to their decision or how to answer the question of what to drink. Think back to the last social gathering you attended. How much did your best friend drink? How about your girlfriend? What about your coworker or your neighbor? Odds are, you have no idea. You are likely to be more sensitive because you think all eyes are on you.

I recommend preparing a short response for the social, work, or family situations you will face. It may be helpful to tell a close friend or family member that you have changed your drinking patterns so that they can run interference for you. If your in-laws are big drinkers, ask your spouse to talk to them to make sure there are no uncomfortable moments, or bring your own drink and have it in your hand so that you avoid altogether the question of what to drink.

Here are some statements you can make when people ask you if you would like a drink:

- "No, thank you."
- "No, I'm not pregnant; I just feel like having a soda."
- "I'm saving my calories for dinner."
- "Alcohol and I no longer mix."
- "I'm trying to lose this belly."
- "Not drinking is my New Year's resolution."
- "I'm giving up alcohol for Lent."
- "Oh, I've already got something."
- "I'm the designated driver."
- "Yeah, rehab is for quitters!"
- "I'm doing a challenge."
- "My doctor wants me to lose a few pounds."
- "I'm on probation."
- "I'm watching my sugar level."
- "My doctor is monitoring my A1C levels."
- "I just got my Medicare card. It says I can't drink anymore!"

- "It's only 1 p.m." (during football season)
- "It makes me sick."
- "I've had my share."

Jokes work well to put everyone at ease. Additionally, you can always speak the simple truth or order a mocktail. Use the one-liner you are most comfortable with. Practice saying it out loud before you arrive at your destination. In this way, you will feel more prepared when you are confronted with a drinking situation, thus avoiding an awkward moment for you as well as your host. If you set the tone of being relaxed and comfortable, the people around you will respond positively. You may also want to devise a signal with the person you are with to let them know when it is time to go. I also suggest this for friends and couples who just want to go home early!

My one-liner is:

_____

My signal to my support person is:

_____

INTERESTING INFO: Do you know how many calories you are drinking? Even light beers have about 100 calories per serving. If you drink 6 beers, you are consuming more than 25 percent of your daily recommended calorie intake. You would have to eat 25 percent less food to make up for the calories taken in on a drinking day. The average glass of wine has 120 calories. A 12-ounce margarita can have 680 calories. Drink 3 and you don't get to eat today, although I do not recommend that.

ANOTHER ROUND OF CHAPTER 8
Moderate Drinking Plan

- Fill out your moderate drinking plan and share it with someone who will support you as well as keep you accountable.
- Be prepared to deal with the emotional aspects of returning to drinking.
- Monitor your amount, intent, impact, and frequency of drinking.
- Revise your plan as your lifestyle changes.
- Use tools to monitor the number of drinks you have at any one time.
- Utilize tangible reminders.
- Practice a one-liner for when you are asked if you want a drink.

Chapter 9

How Do I Maintain This?

This chapter focuses on how to maintain your current drinking plan. If you have developed a moderate drinking plan, these realities will help you determine whether your plan is working for you and prevent you from relapsing by returning to unhealthy alcohol use. If you have decided upon sobriety, these next few pages can guide you in how to be aware of relapse warning signs that you may drink again. I have included excerpts from my handbook *Relapse Reality: Understanding Myths about Relapse in Dual Diagnosis Treatment* as a further tool to aid in your recovery.

First, take the Relapse Reality Quiz to see what you currently believe about relapse. The answers are provided in the following pages. Just as there is a lot of misinformation about ways to deal with problem drinking, there is also much misinformation about recovery.

RELAPSE REALITY QUIZ:

Understanding Myths about Relapse in Dual Diagnosis Treatment

DEFINE RELAPSE:

_____

Answer true or false:

1. If you stop the use of a mood-altering substance and then begin using again, you have relapsed.
2. As long as you do not use alcohol or drugs, you are in recovery.
3. Relapse has identifiable signs and symptoms.
4. Relapse happens because you drop out of treatment or stop attending twelve-step meetings.
5. All you need to avoid relapse are willpower and self-discipline.
6. You do not have to hit bottom in order to interrupt a relapse.
7. If you do not remain abstinent, it is because you have not followed your treatment plan.
8. You have to think about relapsing to avoid it.
9. There are no positive addictions.
10. Once you become sober, any use of alcohol or drugs will quickly result in the same destructive patterns that brought you to treatment.

(Copyright 2007 Cynthia Turner, LCSW, LSATP)

Defining Relapse

What is relapse? Many people use it to mean "I drank again." However, for our purposes, relapse is defined as follows: *A process of thoughts, behaviors, patterns, and emotions that can lead back to the original problem.*

It is important to note that a person can relapse not only with mood-altering substances, but also with mental health issues. The concepts you learn will help you deal not only with relapses with drugs or alcohol, but also with mental health issues or other unhealthy behaviors like overeating, anger management, cigarette smoking, and other such things. Whenever you see terms relating to drug or alcohol use, you can easily substitute them for mental health issues or other areas in which you struggle. While sobriety often refers to someone who has chosen to be completely abstinent from alcohol, the same theories also apply to someone following a moderate drinking plan.

One of the most important words in the definition of relapse is *process*. A process is an identifiable pattern. This is significant because once we identify the pattern we can then interrupt it and return to a healthier place. We will examine myths about relapse and counter with *relapse reality*. It is important to do so because living our lives based upon myths will likely lead to future problems and negative consequences. With correct information, however, we are more likely to make healthier decisions and experience better outcomes.

Clarifying Myths About Relapse

MYTH #1: If you stop the use of a mood-altering substance and then begin using it again, you have relapsed.

REALITY: Relapse cannot occur until you acknowledge that there is a problem and take active steps to correct it. You may go through several stages before becoming healthy. Identify where you think you are today in your recovery process:

1. Regular use of alcohol
2. Attempt to control amount, frequency, or type of substance
3. Attempt to control use through periods of abstinence
4. Decision to stop using, but no lifestyle changes

5. Decision to change patterns and make the necessary lifestyle changes for long-term health

Often a person's "clean date" and "sobriety date" are different. Many people report that they initially stop using because of external pressure from parents, family, or the court system, or because of their health. However, once they make the choice to change and implement the appropriate lifestyle changes, they become sober. The same is true for people who attempt moderate drinking. They may notice a before-and-after experience. One of my clients who successfully managed moderation by dealing with the reasons for her excessive drinking said that was when she finally started living a full life.

What are the lifestyle changes you have made to support your goal with drinking?

_____

_____

_____

_____

MYTH #2: As long as you do not use alcohol or drugs, you are in recovery.

REALITY: Abstinence is only part of recovery. Remember, being sober is so much more than being clean. People have to make many lifestyle changes: peer relationships, their environment, views of the world, ways to deal with stress, ways to have fun, and so forth. The list is endless, as recovery means different things to different people. The way that I define *recovery* is what we do to stay healthy and maintain balance in our lives.

This myth is especially applicable if you are attempting moderation. You can still be in recovery and drink as long as you are sticking to your moderate drinking plan and not experiencing any consequences.

What does recovery mean for you? Be sure to include the things that are not directly related to alcohol.

_____

_____

_____

_____

MYTH #3: Relapse happens without signs or symptoms.

REALITY: Relapse is a process with identifiable signs and symptoms that occur over a period of days, weeks, or months, not a matter of hours or minutes. The goal is to identify your signs and to train others to recognize them so they can help you interrupt them.

Be aware of *post-acute withdrawal symptoms* (PAWS). These often occur in the first ninety days after ceasing alcohol or drug use. They include a heightened sensitivity to the environment, overreaction to stress, emotional numbness, moodiness, sleep problems, and confusion. These reactions occur for a variety of reasons. They happen in part because of chemical damage to the brain and body, as well as the physical and psychological strain of the detoxification process.

You will need to learn how to do many things without the aid of alcohol, including dealing with emotions like anger, stress, depression, and anxiety, while learning new ways to have fun and relate to people. Being aware of what is occurring can be helpful, as well as knowing that the discomfort is temporary and will get better with time and the development of new coping skills. Remember also the theory that when chemical use starts, emotional development often slows down or stops. Many people report that the appearance of new or reemerging emotions overwhelms them. This is why having a good support network and utilizing new coping skills are so important.

Another way to manage PAWS and the flood of emotions is through diet, exercise, and stress management. From these three, select the area that you most struggle with and focus on it during the week. You should get into the habit now so that you can do so when you have less active support.

Identify concrete, measurable ways for you to know that you have achieved your goal of better diet, exercise, or stress management.

_____

_____

_____

_____

MYTH #4: Relapse happens because you drop out of treatment or stop attending twelve-step meetings.

REALITY: While these activities can increase the odds for sobriety or a better relationship with alcohol, a cause-and-effect correlation does not necessarily exist between them. People can be in treatment or going to meetings and still be misusing alcohol or demonstrating other unhealthy behaviors. When people relapse, more likely they are not appropriately utilizing their supports. Each person will need to identify a recovery plan. The time to do it is when you are healthy, thinking clearly, and have an active support system in place.

Hopefully, this book has shown you that many factors go into deciding whether total abstinence or moderation is appropriate for you. One of my goals was to demonstrate that there are numerous paths to recovery. You have to find the right fit for you and your situation.

Think about who is in your support system. It should include friends, family, people in your community, and professionals. Each person may have something different to offer, and you want several people to turn to in case you cannot reach one when you are in crisis. In the space below, write down the names of these people and their numbers. This way you will have them even if you lose your cell phone!

NAME: _____

NUMBER: _____

MYTH #5: Relapse can be prevented with willpower and self-discipline.

REALITY: Willpower is an important part of recovery, but it is only one component. You need knowledge of what is happening to you, especially because the first phase of relapse often is denial. This is significant because if you are pretending that there is no problem, willpower will do nothing to change your unhealthy behavior. You first need to acknowledge the presence of a problem. You need information on what to do when you are in the relapse process, and you need a support system to confront your denial and help you get healthy again.

What is the best way for people to confront you? Does it make a difference whether the problem is with substance use, mental health, or some other issue?

_____

_____

_____

_____

MYTH #6: When you relapse, it means that you have not yet hit bottom.

REALITY: The belief behind the concept of "hitting bottom" is that life has to be at the worst possible point before a person will take the steps to get better. The reality is that you need to recognize that you are experiencing some symptoms before you will seek help. It's the same as recognizing a symptom like a fever or a sore throat before going to see a doctor.

People often seek treatment because of outside pressures—family, court, or poor work or school performance. It takes time to recognize and own the problem, especially if you have been under the influence for a long time. This is why one component to successfully implementing a moderate drinking plan is being substance free for four months. Remember, PAWS can take ninety days to dissipate, and you need time to learn how to do day-to-day activities without using.

Too much pain is not healthy. Your goal is to recognize the symptoms of relapse and get help before your situation gets very bad again. This is why it is so important to have a prevention plan in place, rather than just an emergency action plan. It is easier to prevent a crisis than to resolve one.

Review the areas you have made improvements in, and appraise the obstacles that could hinder your recovery. The analogy of leaving a back door open in a house is applicable here. You may secure your home by locking the front doors and closing all the windows, but if you leave a back door open, unwanted people can still get in. "Back doors" in the recovery process could include keeping extra alcohol in the house "for guests," not telling friends and family that you have changed drinking patterns, or holding on to unhealthy reminders from your drinking days, like shot glasses or empty liquor bottles.

Remember, if you happen to drink excessively again or fall back into unhealthy patterns, you simply lose your clean date. You do not lose all the information you have gained. It is merely an opportunity to reevaluate your moderate drinking or recovery plan.

What back doors do you need to close?

_____

_____

MYTH #7: If you do not remain abstinent from mood-altering substances or problem behaviors, it is because you have not followed your treatment plan.

REALITY: Treatment is not the only tool in having a healthier relationship with alcohol. You need different things at various times in your life. You might have a coexisting mental health disorder like depression, anxiety, bipolar disorder, or ADHD that needs specialized treatment. Additionally, you may have a complicated home life or difficulties with a job, relationship, or school that need to be addressed. Treatment and recovery should be individualized to your needs, and your support system should be incorporated into the plan.

How do you define treatment success? Is it just remaining abstinent from alcohol? It should not be. You have likely made improvements in your home, academic, or job life; put yourself in healthier situations; and cultivated different friends. You are probably involved in many other activities in your day-to-day life. A more realistic goal in your attempt to remain permanently or temporarily abstinent is progress, not perfection.

A relapse isn't just about the alcohol. It is simply a signal that something in your recovery is not working. It can be a powerful experience of learning what not to do, identifying the areas you need to work on, and reinforcing the need to put real effort into recovery. The hope is to decrease the frequency, duration, and impact of the relapse.

Think back to one of your relapses. What did you learn from it?

_____

_____

_____

_____

MYTH #8: Thinking about relapse will make it happen.

REALITY: The opposite is actually true. If you do not think about the possibility of relapse, you are likely to place yourself in higher-risk situations. Think about why you fasten a seatbelt. When you click it, do you assume you are going to be in an accident? No, you do it to protect yourself, just in case. The same concept applies to paying attention to your environment and the choices you make concerning drinking. You need to be aware of your thought processes so that if a risky situation does come up, you are better prepared to deal with it. If you do not think ahead and practice self-awareness, you can be caught off guard and make an impulsive decision that might not yield the best results.

On the flipside, if you are thinking about drinking in excess and see only the good things about it, this indicates a problem. While you may have had fun times while under the influence, the actuality is that your past misuse of alcohol did become a problem in your life. The hope is that when you do reminisce, you will recall the negative things that happened as a result of drinking. Forbidden thinking is not healthy because it tends to increase your cravings. A realistic weighing of the pros and cons relating to alcohol use or other unhealthy behavior tends to yield better results.

What are the consequences from your drinking or unhealthy behavior that you should keep present in your mind? How can you do this?

_____

_____

_____

_____

_____

MYTH #9: There are good addictions that can be used to deal with negative ones.

REALITY: There are no positive addictions. You may believe that you can substitute healthier behaviors for negative ones. You may think it is better to smoke cigarettes than marijuana or to attend hours of AA meetings instead of spending hours in a bar. However, all addictions are bad. They usually indicate a loss of control and imply that the substance or behavior has taken over your thoughts and actions. Actions that are normally considered healthy, like going to church, exercising, and eating better, can have unintended consequences if taken to extremes. If you cannot manage life without the behavior, it is a problem. The new, less destructive behavior is often covering up some other preexisting problem that needs to be addressed. The goal for healthy living is balance. Without it, some area of your life is likely to suffer.

Think about the behaviors you have used to change your drinking patterns. Do you have balance in your life? Which areas still need work?

_____

_____

_____

_____

MYTH #10: Once you have begun recovery, any use of a mood-altering substance will cause immediate problems.

REALITY: Very rarely does one episode of mismanaged alcohol use result in the same destructive pattern as before you made a commitment to change. When it does happen, you may react in different ways. For example, you may try to limit future use, or you may not suffer a significant consequence, so you do it again. If you still do not notice any problems, you may feel comfortable to continue the behavior. Over time, however, the negative patterns that led to the problem drinking in the first place often recur.

Another way you might react is to feel so guilty that you go back to the behavior you tried so hard to discontinue. You may feel hopeless and just give up. The full-blown destructive patterns may then quickly reemerge.

The reality is that if you have had a problem with substances, you are more likely to have the problem again than someone who has not. Think about Russian roulette as an analogy. We all start off with one bullet in our chambers, but because you have had a problem in the past with drugs or alcohol, you are playing the game with at least two or three chambers now filled. If you choose to use mood-altering substances again, you are loading several more chambers. Do you want to play this risky game?

What can you do to reduce your risk? What early warning signs indicate that your drinking is becoming a problem and that you need to get control of it?

_____

_____

_____

_____

Preventing Relapse
TOOLS THAT REDUCE RELAPSE

1. HALT: **H**ungry, **A**ngry, **L**onely, **T**ired. *Halt* translates to "stop" in German. I encourage you to stop, take a moment to reflect, and take action if you need to address any of these areas. If any of them are out of balance, you are more likely to make poor choices.

Hungry: Think about how poorly you feel when you are hungry. When my blood sugar gets low, I get a headache and am irritable and can't concentrate. If you are physically hungry, make sure you refuel with some healthy food. If you know you are going to have a long workday, car ride, or carpool, plan ahead for meals and healthy snacks like fruits, nuts, cheese, yogurt, or protein bars. Don't forget to stay hydrated.

I also believe that *hungry* can refer to how we feel emotionally. If you are bored with your routine, do something to mix it up. Spend time with someone you have not seen in a while, take a car trip, or try an activity you have never done before.

Angry: When we are angry or experiencing negative emotions, we often do not think rationally. When you feel angry, take some time to calm down, talk with a friend, and then address the problem. If it is a chronic issue, break it down into manageable tasks. Just taking even one step forward can make you feel less hopeless and helpless about a situation.

I also recommend waiting at least two hours and talking to another person before you touch technology. This means no texting, tweeting, e-mailing, or posting. You don't want to put something out in cyberspace that you will regret later.

Lonely: We all experience loneliness at times in our lives. Though we may be surrounded by people, we often are not interacting with them. Despite all of modern technology, many of us are plugged in but not connected. Think about the number of times you have made a problem much worse in your head, turning the situation into a catastrophe. However, once you talked it out, you gained a much more positive perspective. Reach out every day and connect face-to-face with other people. Isolation can be a breeding ground for depression and unhealthy choices.

Tired: When we are physically and emotionally tired, we tend to engage in more negative thinking patterns and interactions. Make sure that you get enough sleep at night. Practice good sleep hygiene. I know *sleep hygiene* is a funny phrase, as if you were a dirty sleeper, but it actually refers to developing habits that make restful sleep more conducive. This includes getting up and going to bed around the same time each day, reducing distractions that interrupt sleep (pets, television, or the phone), monitoring caffeine and sugar intake, managing stressors, and limiting exposure to bright lights, which interrupts the biological process that allows melatonin levels to rise and help us drift off to sleep.

What areas of your life tend to get out of balance? What steps can you take to stay healthy?

_____

_____

_____

_____

2. TANGIBLE REMINDERS: As I described in a previous chapter, tangible reminders are things that we can see, feel, touch, and hold that remind us of the changes we are trying to make in our lives regarding alcohol. I recommend keeping reminders in convenient areas such as on your bathroom mirror, on your physical person, in your car, on your phone, and in your workspace. You may want to have both positive and negative reminders to help keep you focused and accountable.

What tangible reminders will you use? Where will you put them?

_____

_____

_____

_____

3. DAILY CHECKS: I encourage you to pick a specific time each day to reflect on your mood, goals, and achievements. Notice that I did not say to look at where you screwed up. Most of us do this to

ourselves anyway, agonizing over what we said or did or didn't do. Classic behavioral reinforcement notes that the behaviors we pay attention to are the ones that get reinforced. Think about that. If all we focus on is what we did wrong, we will keep doing it. But if we look at our successes, we can figure out how to build upon them and will be much happier as a result.

You have a lot more influence over your mood than you realize. Be kinder to yourself in your head. I bet you would never say aloud to another person the things you say about yourself in your head.

Pick a specific time each day to reflect. Some people choose times such as when they are on their way home from work, when they exercise, or when they shower. However, you may not do these activities every day. Haven't you ever had a lazy weekend where you just didn't feel like washing your hair or shaving?

I suggest reflecting when you brush your teeth, something you likely do every day. It takes just a few moments. If you are experiencing a negative emotion, consider proactive ways of dealing with the issue. See if your HALT is in balance. If not, what do you need to do to fix it?

Another daily check to perform is scaling. No, that's not how much you weigh, but how you feel. On a scale of 1 to 10, with 10 being the best day ever and 1 being the worst, where are you today? If you are anywhere from a 7 to a 10, identify those factors that helped create this feeling and repeat them if they are healthy behaviors. If you are below a 4, it might be important to reach out to a friend or a professional. It is completely normal to have a bad day occasionally, sometimes for no apparent reason. But if the bad days continue for more than a week, try to identify the stressor and what you can do to correct it. If the bad days last for more than two weeks or start affecting your activities of daily living, it may be time to seek therapy.

Some people like to keep a journal or a mood tracker. There are also many great apps on smartphones that can help you with this.

Note that you are not comparing yourself to anyone but yourself. Ask yourself, "Am I feeling better or worse today than I did yesterday?" If you track your numbers, thoughts, and feelings, you may notice trends and patterns. That way you can identify the triggers that lead to negative moods and increase the actions that prompt the healthy ones.

What daily check can you use? When will you perform it?

_____

_____

_____

_____

4. WEEKLY CHECKS: Performing weekly checks is very important at the beginning of your abstinence and/or once you have implemented your moderate drinking plan. Again, I recommend selecting a specific day and time to review your goals with your support person. In the first few months, this may be a therapist, support group, or online posting. Eventually you may transition to a friend, partner, or other support person. If you have a committed day, person, and time scheduled, you are more likely to be prepared to review your successes and struggles. Additionally, if you don't show up, your support person will come looking for you to keep you accountable.

I recommend "training" the person you choose as your support person. Let him or her know what your goals are, how to support and confront you, and what signs to watch for. You want that person to give you constructive criticism, not just be critical. It's also important that they have your best interests in mind, not trying to enforce their own agenda. For these reasons, many people consult a professional in the beginning stages of making a change.

*Who is your support person? How can you contact him/her? When will you
meet with him or her?*

_____

_____

_____

_____

5. MONTHLY ACTIVITY: I suggest picking a specific day each month
for a planned activity such as meeting with your counselor, attending an
AA meeting, driving by the courthouse where you were sentenced for
your DUI, or reviewing your moderate drinking plan with your support
person. If you merely say you will do it once a month, you may not
follow through, but if you pick a date that is significant to you, like
the anniversary of your last drink or the date you implemented your
moderate drinking plan, and share it with your support person, you will
be much more likely to stick to it.

What is your monthly activity?

_____

_____

_____

_____

6. OTHER: What are some other tools that you can use to adhere to
your moderate drinking plan and reduce relapses?

_____

_____

_____

_____

ANOTHER ROUND OF CHAPTER 9
How Do I Maintain This?

- Relapse is a process of thoughts, behaviors, and emotions that can lead you back to problem behavior.
- Relapse is a process, and there are patterns that can be identified and therefore interrupted.
- Understanding the many myths about relapse can help you define a healthier and more successful reality in sticking to sobriety or a moderate drinking plan.
- HALT stands for *hungry, angry, lonely,* and *tired.* Identify what is out of balance in your life and take steps to correct it.
- Tangible reminders are things that you can see, feel, hold, and touch that help you remember why you made a change to your drinking patterns.
- Practicing daily, weekly, and monthly checks will help you be more successful in achieving your drinking goals.

INTERESTING INFO: Most drunk-driving fatalities involve people whose blood-alcohol concentration is at least .15 percent or more. There is good reason for the higher jail-sentencing guidelines when the driver's BAC is twice the legal limit of .08 percent that applies in most states.

Chapter 10

Paths To Recovery

As noted throughout this book, there are many paths to recovery. I have often found that the more supports people have, the better successes they experience. You may have heard some of the terms below and wondered what they were. I think television and movies tend to focus on rehab and AA meetings, often making a parody of them, but there are many other types of treatment available. It is important to figure out the level of care appropriate for you.

When your life has spun out of control and you finally decide to get help, it can be overwhelming. You look on the Internet and see many sometimes conflicting and often confusing clinical terms. Then you call your insurance company, and they give you a few names and numbers of people or facilities that may not even call you back. Many people get so stressed by the process of seeking help that they give up, mistakenly thinking that if help is this hard to find, it may not be worth it.

In the following pages, I describe some of the most common types of alcohol treatment that are available, going from most restrictive to least restrictive.

Detox

Detox stands for "detoxification." You read in previous chapters about the potentially fatal consequences of alcohol withdrawal. If you are experiencing symptoms of alcohol withdrawal, you will need detox. You will be in a hospital-type room, given some type of benzodiazepine, and regularly have your vitals checked. Detox often lasts from three to seven days. It can be done in a regular hospital setting, but I suggest having it done in a facility dedicated to alcohol and drug treatment. In this way, specifically trained professionals can help you manage the medical as well as emotional impact stemming from withdrawal. These facilities are also often connected to a continuum of care for alcohol dependence. Detox is not therapy. It is medically managing symptoms of alcohol withdrawal. Keep in mind that detox is often only the first step in a long recovery process.

Rehab

Rehab is for quitters! Okay, I'm trying to be funny, but that is exactly the goal of rehab programs. Rehab is often a twenty-eight or thirty-day program, but it can be sixty, ninety, or even more days. Sadly, insurance companies and personal finances often dictate how long someone can remain at this level of care. We do know that the longer someone remains in treatment, the better the chances of long-term success.

Rehab is for you if you want to and are unable to quit using on your own, need a medical detoxification, face numerous stressors that you have been unable to handle effectively while in your home, and need to be away from your environment to get healthy. During rehab, you live in the facility, and the majority of therapeutic services are provided in the location. Some facilities have a detox unit on site so that you can go "bed to bed" without a break in service.

Rehab tends to be less like a hospital and more like a dorm. You will typically participate in both group and individual therapy, twelve-step meetings, education, and various other forms of treatment, which might include equine therapy, yoga, meditation, exercise, and other activities. There are numerous excellent facilities located all across the country. A therapist or interventionist can help you find one that works for you and your finances, family, employer, and mental health needs.

Interventionist

Certain television shows have popularized interventions. The job of an interventionist is to identify the appropriate people in your life who can motivate you into seeking treatment and aftercare. The interventionist helps your family and friends present their concerns to help facilitate a change in your life. He or she is a trained professional with connections in the recovery community and can actually take the person to rehab. The use of an interventionist can be a costly process and should be used only after all other options have failed or a person's life is in danger without treatment.

Keep in mind that therapists specializing in substance-use disorders are often well connected to the various types of treatment available, not only in your area, but also across the country. There are times when general practitioners refer people to me for an assessment of the most appropriate type of treatment. Part of my evaluation is to triage the issues, determine whether I am able to provide treatment, and refer the client to a higher level of care if warranted. I also collaborate with family members and other professionals to create an individualized treatment plan for the person's needs. Sometimes I am the right fit, but sometimes the person needs something more or different from what I can provide.

IOP

The next step after rehab is usually an intensive outpatient program (IOP) or some form of transitional living. IOP is typically for nine hours a week, three hours at a time. It generally consists of group and individual therapy, education, and twelve-step meetings. There is then often a step-down of continuing care to include individual and family therapy and self-help groups. IOP may be for you if you are struggling with obtaining alcohol-free days, lack structure in your day, or want to focus more on sobriety than on moderation.

Transitional Living

If you have completed a residential stay (rehab), some form of transitional living may be recommended. Certain terms describing transitional living are often used interchangeably, but they can actually mean very different things. Let's look at two of them: *sober living* and a *halfway house.*

Sober living is for people who are not ready to return home and need help with obtaining a job, finding housing, developing structure, and repairing relationships. Sober-living facilities are usually private residences within the county and are paid for privately, through insurance, with government assistance, or a combination of the three. The most consistent expectation is that in order to participate, you must remain abstinent. Sober living is for the person who has had a more severe alcohol problem and is unable to return to his or her previous living situation. Many residences have a house manager, expect residents to share in chores, offer twelve-step meetings, assist with employment, and perform other helpful functions.

A halfway house is for inmates who have been released from prison and need assistance reintegrating into the community. These tend to be government funded. Before entering any facility, be sure to check out how it is run. There are a number of types, lengths of stay allowed, as well as expectations to be followed.

Co-Occurring or Dual Diagnosis

These terms can be used interchangeably. They refer to treatment that takes into account both mental health issues as well as substance-use-disorders challenges. It is important to note that it was not until the 1980s that providers began integrating both issues and thus receiving education that enabled them to treat both in the same facility. Don't be afraid to ask a professional any questions you may have about his or her training; you need to make sure they are able to help you. The best therapy will also involve your support system. Just as you are making lifestyle changes, so will they in response to you.

Group Therapy

There are many different types of group therapies. Speak to the group leader to understand who usually attends the group, what the group expectations are, what the goals are, and what the format will be.

There are *open*, *closed*, and *didactic* (fancy way of saying "educational") formats. *Open* means people may enter the group at any time. This format is helpful for new members because they share the experience of others who are also new to recovery as well as receive hope and advice from members who have been successful. Those who are in the middle of the process are reminded of what it was like in the early stages of the struggle, have the opportunity to work on their goals, and have hope for closure. Those who are ready to transition out of the group share their successes with others, which reinforces them as they prepare to move to the next stage of their recovery. My current adult dual diagnosis group has been running for over ten years. Members have said that they benefit from being exposed to people with varying issues and points and goals for their recovery.

Closed groups can have two meanings. In therapy, a closed group usually means that all members start and end at the same time, sometimes with a set number of sessions. This type of group is usually more conducive to educational purposes, but it can also foster a greater feeling of connectedness among the members, since all are going through the same process. Closed groups also give members a chance to learn about a specific topic or topics and allow for more cohesion. In twelve-step meetings, a closed group is only for the person in recovery, not professionals, friends, or families of addicts.

As noted above, *didactic groups* usually teach a specific set of skills. They are often not as emotionally draining because participants are more passive, listening to an instructor. They tend to be utilized in early treatment when learning new tools is important.

Interestingly, when I recommend group therapy to my clients, I receive the most resistance. People say they are shy, don't want to talk in front of strangers, are afraid they will have nothing in common with members in the group, or do not want to hear about other people's problems. It is hard for them to imagine how a group works and to grasp that their defenses will tumble and they will share intimate things they never thought they would with people they never would have spoken to outside of the group. Group therapy is even great in the times when members conflict with each other.

The reason for this is that group is like a microcosm. How people function in a group is typically a reflection of who they are in the real world. Groups are a healthy and safe place for people to try out new behaviors and skills as well as work through conflicts with peers. They also receive support and benefit from the perspectives of others who have dealt with a similar issue. Many people report that they feel more understood, better connected, and less isolated when in a group.

Group therapy also has another benefit: it costs less than individual therapy.

Try a group. I guarantee you will be surprised at how much you come to enjoy and value the experience. It doesn't matter if it is a therapy group, a twelve-step meeting, a church-sponsored group, or a peer group. Give it at least three tries; if you don't like it, at least you know there is another resource out there.

Individual Psychotherapy/Counseling

Psychotherapy, *therapy*, and *counseling* also are terms that tend to be interchanged. Psychotherapy is often just called therapy. Therapy and counseling are very similar, and the services often overlap. However, a counselor generally focuses on brief interventions and concentrates on behavior. On the other hand, therapy tends to be longer in nature and focuses on gaining insight to emotional problems. A psychotherapist often has more training and experience than a counselor. Another important difference is that insurance companies often reimburse only for psychotherapy.

A common misconception is that there must be something wrong with a person to seek therapy. However, therapy can help anyone. You do not have to be diagnosed with a mental disorder to benefit from therapy. In fact, my healthiest clients are ones that I see periodically. These are healthy, high-functioning individuals who realize that it is better to prevent a problem than to react to one.

Healthy adults usually have a team of support. We use financial advisors, tax preparers, and personal trainers, so why not use someone who helps keep our minds healthy and offers an unbiased perspective with only our interests at stake? In fact, we in the helping profession refer to the people who come to see us as clients, not patients, because we do not believe they are sick.

Why is it that we sometimes treat our cars better than we treat ourselves? Even the best-engineered automobiles benefit from routine preventative maintenance. We are no different and deserve the same type of care.

Who Does Therapy?

It can be overwhelming to figure out the right person to use as a therapist. There are several types of professionals trained to do therapy. I break it down like this:

- *Psychiatrists* prescribe medication.
- *Psychologists* do testing and research.
- *Licensed professionals* do therapy. I will explain more in a second.

Significant differences exist between the professions; however, all of the disciplines are trained to do therapy. I encourage you not to focus on the type of therapy a clinician provides, because really good clinicians tend to be eclectic. This means that the professional will adapt the therapy to the approach that works best for you and also change therapy and techniques as you focus on different issues.

There are too many types of therapies and styles to describe all of them. After being in the field for over twenty years, I can tell you, however, that every few years a new type of therapy comes along with a new acronym, book, training, and certification. Certainly, some of these have proven better for treating certain issues, but often the new therapies are very similar to what is out there already, only with a new twist. Do what works for you and don't let anyone tell you that you are not seeing the right person if you are making positive lifestyle changes and thinking and acting healthier.

Which One Should You Pick?

Almost any therapist can treat the *walking wounded or worried well,* terms that describe people who are experiencing general issues with a relationship or a mood disorder like depression or anxiety. All therapists are trained in treating the most common issues and disorders, but it is important to check the clinician's credentials when dealing with more complex issues that affect many life areas, such as addictions, eating disorders, or severe mental illness.

Most important of all is your relationship with the therapist. If you feel like you are getting help and making positive changes in your life, it is probably a good fit. If you feel like the therapist doesn't understand you, is not helping you, and you dread going to therapy, try someone else. Just as in a romantic relationship, you will know it when it clicks. Remember, what worked with one counselor may not work with another issue.

Be aware that all doctors are not the same. For example, Dr. Jones, MD, is different from Dr. Jones, PhD. The first one is medically trained, which includes completing four years of undergraduate study, four years of medical school, and an additional three to seven years before becoming license eligible. The second one is a doctor of philosophy. This is a little confusing because having a PhD does not mean that a person is necessarily versed in philosophy; a better explanation is that PhDs possess a love of wisdom. PhDs have completed extensive undergraduate and graduate coursework and have often completed a dissertation, a scholarly project that demonstrates independent contributions to their field.

It gets even more confusing with the doctor title. In most states, even if you have a PhD, you still have to earn a license to conduct private practice or be reimbursable by insurance companies. Each state has its own licensing criteria.

This brings us to other licensed professionals. Some have many letters after their names; this is important because while these clinicians are not called "doctor," they have earned undergraduate and graduate degrees in the helping profession, completed several internships or residencies, completed at least two years of clinical supervision under a trained clinician, and passed a licensing exam. They also receive ongoing education and maintain professional standards.

Each state has a variety of names for the licenses. For example, I am a licensed clinical social worker (LCSW) and a licensed substance abuse treatment practitioner (LSATP). Just across the border from my state of Virginia, in Maryland, I would be called an LCSW-C, and in the District of Columbia, an LiCSW. Having a license is important because it means that insurance will reimburse for services rendered and that the clinician has undergone significant education, training, and experience.

There are also a variety of substance-use certifications. Some are for professionals and some are for those in recovery, people who receive education and supervision in order to help others who struggle with an addiction like theirs. Some of these people talk about their recovery with clients, while others keep it more private. Explore and choose whatever works best for you. Many clinicians have websites that share information about themselves and their philosophies. You can also use a variety of search engines to find professionals in your area. A professional's license is usually verified in order to be listed on many of these sites.

Over the last fifty years, research has found that the number one reason people are able to make change in therapy is the strength of the therapeutic alliance. Simply put, the therapist and client agree on the goals and have a bond between them that facilitates reaching those goals. The therapist should create a safe space without judgment to set goals and work towards the changes the client wants to make. These are the same qualities needed in an effective support person.

Whatever discipline you choose, it is most important that you feel comfortable with your therapist. You will be entrusting that person with some of your deepest secrets and trusting that they will help guide you. You should feel like your therapist has your best interests in mind, but you don't have to agree with everything they say. In fact, sometimes your therapist may actually want you to get frustrated or angry. That may signify that they have challenged you in a session.

The therapist's job is not to make you feel good. That is what friends do. The therapist's job is to help you find solutions to your problems and turn insights into action.

EAP

Many larger companies offer a service called an *employer assistance program*. This is a work-based intervention program designed to identify and assist employees in resolving personal problems, including alcohol misuse, which may adversely affect the employee's performance. Check with your employer to see if you have access to an EAP. These programs are voluntary and offer free and confidential assessments, short-term referrals, and follow-up services. They can also connect you to appropriate treatment if you need more assistance.

Medication

PCPs (primary care physicians), PAs (physician assistants), and NPs (nurse practitioners) are all able to write prescriptions. However, a psychiatrist is usually the best person to prescribe psychotropic medications to manage any underlying mental health concerns, because they have specialty training in this field. Before going on these medications, though, first try to see if you can make changes to your physical environment. Did you know that exercise has been found to be as effective as an antidepressant in treating depression? Can you cut down on your caffeine intake to decrease your anxiety? Would you have more energy if you slept an extra hour a day? Are you eating a well-balanced diet to fuel your body and mind? Are there other ways to manage your stress? Keep in mind that no one is perfect. Sometimes good is good enough.

Change what you can in your environment, and then see if you can develop coping skills to deal with the rest. If you are still experiencing symptoms or if those symptoms get in the way of your day-to-day life and responsibilities, it may be time to consult a professional for medication.

You should also be aware of the excellent advances in medications for the treatment of more severe alcohol use. Let me discuss a few. *Antabuse* (disulfiram) works by blocking an enzyme involved in metabolizing alcohol intake. It will make a person violently ill if consumed with any form of alcohol. This is the medication I recommend the least. First, it has to be taken on a daily basis. If a person wants to drink, he or she can simply stop taking the pill for several days and then plan a relapse. (I am not endorsing this!) Additionally, some clients need to drink so badly that they will endure the negative effects of the drug and just keep drinking—not a pleasant experience.

A number of my clients have had success with *Revia* (naltrexone). This is an opiate antagonist that basically blocks the high generated from drinking. It works by reducing cravings for alcohol as well as decreasing its pleasurable effects.

As a man named Bob explained:

I saw the beer truck drive by and . . . nothing—I didn't even want it. It could have been a vegetable truck. I didn't even care. When people on television shows are drinking, I no longer feel like I have to change the channel. I can go out to dinner with my wife and not feel like I want to have a cocktail before dinner anymore.

Vivitrol is an injectable form of naltrexone. It has been on the market for about ten years and is a good choice for those who struggle with taking daily medication. One downside is that it costs about ten times as much the pill form, and insurance does not always cover it. The Vivitrol shot is also helpful for those who are wavering in their commitment to total abstinence and can be beneficial because they do not have to think about taking a pill every day.

Campral (acamprosate) restores the chemical imbalances within the brain caused by alcohol use. It is believed to help the brain begin working normally again and reduces the physical and emotional distress that may be experienced when a person stops drinking. Campral is appropriate only for those who have already stopped drinking and are choosing long-term sobriety.

Please note that the most effective recovery results from having as many supports as possible. Medication should be viewed as only one of many tools for recovery, not the only one.

Self-Help Groups

There are numerous self-help groups available. Below is a list of some of the most common ones for people looking to achieve sobriety or to drink in moderation.

- *Alcoholics Anonymous (AA)*: The only requirement for participation in Alcoholics Anonymous is the desire to stop drinking. Meetings are free and held all over the world. In addition to meetings, the program offers sponsorship from a member who is established in recovery and serves new members as their own personal recovery guide. The program also offers fellowship with others who have experienced similar struggles with alcohol. Participants tend to reap the best benefits from the program by working the twelve steps. This helps them take stock of where they are in their recovery journey and provides tools for sobriety. AA has been around since the 1930s. I do not recommend attending AA if your goal is moderation.
- *Celebrate Recovery (CR)*: CR is a Christ-based approach founded by pastors Rick Warren and John Baker. It is aimed at all

"hurts, habits, and hang-ups" and offers help for those suffering from drug, alcohol, or sex addiction; eating disorders; anxiety disorders; or sexual abuse. The program utilizes eight recovery principles based on the Sermon on the Mount.

- *HAMS*: HAMS stands for "harm reduction, alcohol abstinence, and moderation support." It is a free support and informational group for people who want less destructive drinking habits. They support the goals of safer drinking, reduced drinking, or quitting. Participants choose the goal and may switch it at any time.

- *Moderation Management (MM):* MM is "a behavioral change program and national support network for people concerned about their drinking and who desire to make positive lifestyle changes." It is the first moderation-based support group and is run by members. It encourages individuals to accept responsibility for maintaining their own recovery path. MM promotes early recognition of risky drinking so that moderate drinking is more likely to be achieved.

- *Narcotics Anonymous (NA)*: NA is a nonprofit fellowship of men and women for whom drugs have become a problem. NA's vision is for "every addict in the world to have the chance to experience our message in his or her own language and culture and find the opportunity for a new way of life." It is the second largest twelve-step organization. The only requirement is a desire to stop using drugs. Again, I do not recommend NA if moderation is your goal.

- *SMART Recovery*: SMART Recovery is a self-empowering addiction-recovery support group. SMART stands for "self-management and recovery training." It has been around for twenty years. Participants learn to use tools based on the latest scientific research and attend self-help groups. SMART offers a four-point program with tools and techniques for each. This includes building and maintaining motivation; coping with urges; managing thoughts, feelings, and behaviors; and living a balanced life. SMART is typically for those wanting to achieve abstinence but people wanting to try moderation are still invited to participate.

• *Women for Sobriety Inc. (WFS)*: WFS is a nonprofit organization dedicated to helping women overcome alcoholism and other addictions. WFS is the first national program for women alcoholics and is based on the New Life Program. This includes thirteen acceptance statements that provide women a new way of life through a new way of thinking. WFS believes that image precedes actions and encourages women to practice the positive statements so they can have positive thoughts, which will lead to positive actions. WFS is primarily an online forum with message boards and chats run by moderators.

The list I have provided of the paths to recovery is by no means exhaustive. There are numerous smart phone apps, podcasts, books, and meditations that may assist you. My goal was to give you a snapshot and explanation of the available treatment options. I know that when you make that first call to a therapist, you are probably in crisis. Finding the right type of help should not add to your stress. If a certain therapist is not the right fit for you, they should help you locate someone who is. A good therapist will know the resources that are available in your area.

ANOTHER ROUND OF CHAPTER 10
Paths to Recovery

- There are numerous ways for problem drinkers to get help.
- Detox, rehab, and IOPs are usually first steps of treatment for alcoholics.
- After the alcoholic has achieved at least a month of abstinence, sober living, twelve-step meetings, group and individual therapy, and medication may be added to the treatment plan.
- Drinkers experiencing problems often do well with a combination of education, support groups, and/or therapy. They usually do not need the higher levels of treatment described above.
- The longer people participate in an active recovery program, the better their chances for success.
- The type of discipline used by a therapist is less important than the client's therapeutic relationship with the therapist.
- Numerous support groups are available to help with total abstinence from alcohol or developing and managing a moderate drinking plan.

INTERESTING INFO: Did you know that the Serenity Prayer did not come from AA? The prayer was actually written as a response to the evils of Nazi Germany. It was written by the theologian Reinhold Niebuhr, a first-generation German-American, about the ethical predicament of German immigrants in the United States, who were safe from persecution but powerless against Hitler. Niebuhr reportedly delivered the original version at the conclusion of a sermon in Union Church in Massachusetts. However, even this is much debated. There are several versions of the prayer that date back to fourteenth-century England or even to Roman philosophy in AD 480. Nonetheless, the Serenity Prayer is a source of comfort for many throughout the world, not just at AA meetings.

God grant us the serenity to
accept the things we cannot change,
Courage to change the things we can,
And wisdom to know the difference.

Last Call

Congratulations! Very rarely do we get praise as adults. So here it is: I am proud of you! You have put active effort into helping yourself be the best version of you that you can be. It can be very hard to look at your shortcomings and even harder to make changes to them.

I wish you success with your drinking plan, whatever you have chosen. I hope you found a relationship with alcohol that works for you and your family. Please know that there are all types of people out there, including nondrinkers who still have fun and are not bored. It takes work to live a balanced life, but you are worth it.

If you would like to share your success story with me, I would love to hear it! Just send it to me at cturner@canikeepdrinking.com.

If you are still struggling, please know that there are many professionals, tools, self-help groups, and people who have developed a healthier relationship with alcohol. Don't give up. It may take several different types of treatment and effort to maintain change. Overcoming difficulties with drinking is one of the hardest changes you can undertake, but there is hope. The journey of recovery will take you many places you may not expect, but you will be happier and healthier along the way.

References

American Psychiatric Association. 2013. *Diagnostic and Statistical Manual of Mental Disorders*, 5th ed. Washington, DC.

Anderson, Kenneth G., PhD. CreateSpace: 2010. *How to Change Your Drinking: A Harm Reduction Guide to Alcohol*, 2nd ed. The HAMS Harm Reduction Network.

Callo, Vince. April 25, 2014. "States with the Most Drunk Driving."

Centers for Disease Control and Prevention (CDC). "Alcohol-Related Disease Impact" (ARDI). Atlanta, GA: CDC.

Denning, Patt, Little, Jeanne, and Glickman, Adina. New York: The Guilford Press. 2003. Over the Influence: The Harm Reduction Guide for Managing Drugs and Alcohol.

Dept. of Transportation (US), National Highway Traffic Safety Administration (NHTSA). Traffic Safety Facts 2013 Data: Alcohol-Impaired Driving. Washington (DC): NHTSA; 2014 [cited 2015 May 18].

Dodes, Lance, MD and Zachary Dodes. Beacon Press: 2014. *The Sober Truth:*
Debunking the Bad Science Behind 12-Step Programs and the Rehab Industry.

Drake, Robert E., Kim T. Mueser, and Mary F. Brunette. "Management of Persons with Co-occurring Severe Mental Illness and Substance Use Disorder: Program Implications." *World Psychiatry*. 2007. Oct. 6(3): 131–136.

Esser M. B., S. L Heeden, D. Kanny, R. D. Brewer, J. C. Gfroer, and T. S. Naimi. 2014. "Prevalence of Alcohol Dependence Among US Adult Drinkers, 2009–2011." *Preventing Chronic Disease.*

Ferri, FF. Delirium tremens. In: Ferri FF, ed. Ferri's Clinical Advisor 2015. 1st ed. Philadelphia: PA Elsevier Mosby; 2015:p. 357.

Fletcher, Anne. June 18, 2015. Living with Addiction, roundtable discussion. "New Study Reveals Sharp Spike in Alcohol Use Disorders."

Glaser, Gabrielle. New York: Simon & Schuster. 2013. *Her Best Kept Secret: Why Women Drink and How They Can Regain Control.*

Grant, B. F., R. B. Goldstein, T. D. Saha, S. P. Chou, J. Jung, J. Zhang, R. P. Pickering, W. J. Ruan, S. M. Smith, B. Huang, and D. S. Hasin. August 2015. "Epidemiology of DSM-5 Alcohol Use Disorder: Results From the National Epidemiologic Survey on Alcohol and Related Conditions III." *JAMA Psychiatry.*

Hess, Alexander E. M., Thomas C. Frohlich, and Vince Callo. May 15, 2014. "The Heaviest-Drinking Countries in the World."

Hester, Delaney, & Campbell (2011). "ModerateDrinking.com and Moderation Management: Outcomes of a Randomized Clinical Trial with Non-Dependent Problem Drinkers." *Journal of Counseling and Psychology.*

Hester, Delaney, Campbell, and Handmaker. 2009. "A web application for moderation training: initial results of a randomized clinical trial." *Journal of Substance Abuse Treatment*, 37, 266–276.

Horvath, Thomas, PhD. California: Impact Publishers. 2003. *Sex, Drugs, Gambling, & Chocolate: A Workbook for Overcoming Addictions.*

Horvath, Tom, PhD, ABPP. Posted March 25, 2014. "Is AA Harmful?" Practical Recovery Blog.

Horvath, Tom, PhD. Posted August 11, 2014. "To Moderate or to Abstain?" Practical Recovery Blog.

Kellogg, Scott H. and Andrew Tatarsky. 2012. "Re-envisioning Addiction Treatment: A Six Point Plan," *Alcoholism Treatment Quarterly*, 30:1, 109–128, DOI.

Kelly JF, Westerhoff CM. "Does it matter how we refer to individuals with substance-   related conditions? A randomized study of two commonly used terms." *International Journal of Drug Policy.* 2010;21:202-207.

Kilmer, Jason; Palmer, Rebekka S.; Cronce, Jessica M.; Logan, Diane E. January 31, 2012. "Reducing the harms of college student drinking: How Alan Marlatt changed approaches, outcomes, and the field." *Addiction Research and Theory*, 20:3, 227-235.

Logan, D. E. and Marlatt, G. A. (2010), "Harm reduction therapy: a practice-friendly review of research." *Journal of Clinical Psychology.* 66: 201–214.

Mayo Clinic.org. April 24, 2014. "Red Wine and Resveratrol. Good for Your Heart?" Written by Mayo Clinic staff.

Mann, Denise. January 22, 2013. "Alcohol and a Good Night's Sleep Don't Mix." WebMD Health News.

Meier, P. S., M. C. Donmall, P. McEldenuff, C. Barrowclough, and R. F. Heller. June 9, 2006. "The Role of the Early Therapeutic Alliance in Predicting Drug Treatment Dropout." *Drug and Alcohol Dependence.*

"Moderate Drinking Options: Alternatives to Abstinence for Problem Drinkers." Moderatedrinkingoptions.com.

National Council on Alcoholism and Drug Dependence Inc. December 2014. "Facts About Alcohol."

National Institutes of Health: "Understanding Alcohol's Impact on Our Body."

National Institute on Alcohol Abuse and Alcoholism. 2007. *Helping Patients Who Drink Too Much: A Clinician's Guide.*

National Institute on Alcohol Abuse and Alcoholism. April 1992, no.16. "Alcohol Alert: Moderate Drinking."

National Institute on Alcohol Abuse and Alcoholism. December 2014. "Alcohol Facts and Statistics."

National Institute on Drug Abuse: "The Science of Drug Abuse and Addiction." www.drugabuse.com.

Pederson, Traci. November 30, 2014. "Most Problem Drinkers Not Alcohol Dependent."

Project Know. December 2014. "Drug Addiction Statistics-Alcoholism Statistics and Data Sources."

Rennie, S. "Alcohol Answers: Evidence-Based Treatment and Support." www.alcoholanswers.org.

"Rethinking Drinking: Alcohol and Your Health." www.rethinkingdrinking.niaaa.nih.gov.

Saad, Lydia. August 17, 2012. "Majority in U.S. Drink Alcohol, Averaging Four Drinks a Week." *Well Being.*

Saison, Joanna, Melinda Smith, and Jeanne Segal. December 2014. "Substance Abuse and Mental Health." HelpGuide.org.

Satel, Sally and Scott O. Lilienfeld. October 8, 2013. "Addiction and the Brain Disease Fallacy." *Frontiers in Psychiatry.*

Substance Abuse and Mental Health Services Administration. 2013. "Results for the 2012 National Survey on Drug Use and Health: Summary of National Findings." NSDUH Series H-46, HHS Publications No. (SMA) 13-4795. Rockville, MD.

Science Links.com. "Alcohol and the Human Body."

Tatarsky, Andrew. October 2013. "Integrative Harm Reduction Psychotherapy: An Essential Part of Effective Treatment for

Substance Misuse and Other Risky Addictive Behavior" presentation. National Football League Program for Substances of Abuse presentation.

Tatarsky, Andrew and Alan G. Marlatt. 2010. "State of the Art in Harm Reduction Psychotherapy: An Emerging Treatment for Substance Misuse." *Journal of Clinical Psychology*: in Session. Wiley Periodicals Inc.

Voss, Gretchen. October 2014. "A Healthier Pour." Oprah.com.

Washton, Arnold M., PhD. 2008. *Treating Alcohol and Drug Problems in Psychotherapy Practice: Doing What Works.*

Wupperman, Peggilee. October 2013. "The Use of Mindfulness to Treat Problematic Substance Use and Aggression: Strategies and Techniques from Mindfulness and Modification Therapy and Mindfulness-Based Relapse Prevention" presentation. National Football League Program for Substances of Abuse presentation.

Resources

Alcoholics Anonymous: www.aa.org
CR: Celebrate Recovery. Celebraterecovery.com
HAMS: Harm Reduction for Alcohol. www.hamsnetwork.org
Moderate Drinking: Moderatedrinking.org
Moderation Management: www.moderation.org
Mothers Against Drunk Driving: www.madd.org
Narcotics Anonymous: www.na.org
National Institute on Drug Abuse: www.drugabuse.gov
National Institute on Alcohol Abuse & Alcoholism: www.niaaa.nih.gov
SMART Recovery: www.smartrecovery.org
Women for Sobriety: www.womenforsobriety.org

About The Author

Cyndi Turner is a licensed clinical social worker and licensed substance abuse treatment practitioner who has been in the field for over twenty years. She cofounded and is the Clinical Director of Insight Into Action Therapy, a private outpatient therapy practice with two offices in northern Virginia. She codeveloped and facilitates the Dual Diagnosis Recovery Program©. Local courts have qualified her as an expert witness and she provides therapy to players involved with the National Football League Program for Substances of Abuse.

Cyndi is willing to challenge the traditional belief that all drinkers experiencing problems must be alcoholics who need to quit drinking forever. She is a Moderation Management-friendly therapist and is Get SMART FAST certified. She lives in northern Virginia and loves anything to do with sun, sand, beaches, or boats.

A free eBook edition is available with the purchase of this book.

To claim your free eBook edition:

1. Download the Shelfie app.
2. Write your name in upper case in the box.
3. Use the Shelfie app to submit a photo.
4. Download your eBook to any device.

Shelfie

A free eBook edition is available
with the purchase of this print book.

CLEARLY PRINT YOUR NAME ABOVE IN UPPER CASE

Instructions to claim your free eBook edition:
1. Download the Shelfie app for Android or iOS
2. Write your name in **UPPER CASE** above
3. Use the Shelfie app to submit a photo
4. Download your eBook to any device

Print & Digital Together Forever.

Snap a photo   Free eBook   Read anywhere

 Morgan James makes all of our titles available through the Library for All Charity Organizations.

www.LibraryForAll.org

CPSIA information can be obtained
at www.ICGtesting.com
Printed in the USA
LVOW10s1529020317
525947LV00005B/974/P